ROSES IN DECEMBER

The Last Forty Years

The true story of the last 40 years

through the eyes of one, shared by many

but relived by few. In this account, the

feelings echo our common memories of

another time we will not forget.

By Rose Marie Brauer

Blessings –
Rose Marie Brauer

Her first book:
MY NORTH DAKOTA PRAIRIE CHILDHOOD

Published by Gregory Publishers 4425 Crestland Drive St. Louis, Missouri 63121 (314) 389-8054

May 1990: First Edition, First Printing
August 1990: Second Printing
March 1991: Third Printing
June 1993: Fourth Printing
August 1994: Fifth Printing

ISBN 0-9643204-0-1 $15.00

Library of Congress Catalog Card Number: 94-79031

Her second book; a sequel to her first:
ROSES IN DECEMBER: The Last 40 Years

Published by Gregory Publishers
4425 Crestland Drive
St. Louis, Missouri 63121
(314) 389-8054

October 1994: First Edition, First Printing

June 1995: First Edition, Second Printing

Scripture quotations are from the King James Version of the Bible.

Cover: Peace Rose Photography by Joseph W. Bridwell

ISBN: 0-9643204-1-X $15.00

Library of Congress Catalog Card Number: 94-79032

ACKNOWLEDGEMENTS

To my husband Donald Brauer whose courage and loving care have kept me going for 25 years.

To my son Dr. Gregory Oetting who has given me a purpose in life and constant joy.

To my daughter-in-law Amy who loves my son and has given life to their child, my first grandchild, Reid Walter.

To my loyal friends Bob and Lori Duesenberg who have shared their loving companionship for over 40 years.

To Joanne Michael Lanser whose mutual friendship we have cherished for many years.

To Mary O'Brien for her quiet patience in putting this manuscript on computer.

To Marie Schroeder, Betty Guebert, and Dr. Frederick and Lois Danker who assisted me in editing this book, with deepest gratitude.

This book is dedicated to my dear husband Donald E. Brauer, to my precious son Dr. Gregory M. Oetting with deepest love and thanks, to Reid Walter Oetting who arrived in good health during the final editing of this book on November 28, 1993, and to his mother Amy who lovingly cares for the whole family.

****

I dedicate this book to Peace and
Justice for every living being.

CONTENTS

Lord, make me an instrument of your peace
Where there is injury...pardon.
Where there is doubt...faith.
Where there is despair...hope.
Where there is darkness...light.
Where there is sadness.. joy.

O Divine Master, grant that I may not
so much seek to be consoled as to console.
To be understood...as to understand.
To be loved...as to love;
For it is in giving...that we receive,
It is in pardoning...that we are pardoned,
And it is in dying that we are born

to an eternal life.

St France of Assisi

PROLOGUE

As I look out over the softy falling snow, our very first accumulation of the drifting white fluff, I embark on my second book, a sequel to the first, North Dakota Prairie Childhood. Memories of my childhood come rushing through my thoughts. Unforgettable happy times growing up on those beloved North Dakota prairies. Again the mind revives the sadness of seeing my friends Lori Hall Duesenberg, who also came from those familiar plains, and her husband Bob moving to Washington D.C. two years ago. That golden thread woven through our lives these many years severed by the miles.

It seems strange that I feel as compulsive about writing down the last forty years of my life as I did about the first twenty-two. I cannot explain it, but I cannot go on without taking this time to put it on paper. I must go back and relive those years to find the full meaning of my life, my raison d'etre. In Socrates Apology he said the life which is unexamined is not worth living...

They say the mind is selective about what it remembers and how it changes those memories as time passes. We do recall what we really want to remember, and we forget experiences and people we don't really care about. I remember happy times, sad times...all mistily etched in my mind forever. I must bring them forth, give them words, so they remain for future generations. There are specific instances I can remember when someone just mentions an event, an address, or a place. When memories of the past start slipping away yielding to the immediate necessities of the present - like what day it is, what tasks I have to do - there is a fear of losing them. I write down events and places before they vanish completely. This loss of memory is true of the many folks I see in the nursing home which I visit regularly, and true of my former neighbor whose mind and memories are erased forever.

My purse carries another memory bank - and lately, fearing I'd lose it to chance or theft, I've taken care to remember important things within its cavernous walls. At long last I've memorized my social security numbers! However hard I try, names of new people slip away from my memory as fast as I put them in. Is this memory overload, or just the pressure to relieve the mind of the past on these pages? I have kept journals of specific things I want to recall. The pages of this book are the past details which I want my children and grandchildren to know. Many others are curious about who this Rose is, who she was then, and who she is now. These memories are for you. Possibly you too can identify with them.

The events of my first book took place up to the time of my marriage in 1954. These are the 40 years that followed. Looking back over the past forty years is a bit overwhelming. Visualize with me trekking up a steep mountain along a narrow path with thorns and brambles on both sides. The path leads upward to a dangerous precipice backed by a protective wall on one side, but the other is open - a misstep would mean disaster. This vision is my life.

These pages reflect my quest for personal and spiritual growth. This path to wholeness has brought me to an ever increased awareness of my losses. By writing about these events, I relived the truth of where I have been, and what I have suppressed. I grieved for every moment time had not erased, but only left suspended in the recesses of my soul. This truth defines my identity and clarifies my purpose in life.

I have revisited the joys and the sorrows also for those who have struggled in their families these many years. For those who also raised their children as best they could during the "Age of Aquarius," and who wrestle with justice every day of their life.

My purpose in writing this book is for a better understanding and sensitivity between the generations, and for so many with undisclosed pain of the past, to help each other walk in someone else's shoes, and finally, to give hope and a renewed spirit to those who are hurting.

Many of the readers will welcome the use of the King James version in the scripture quotations, our daily source of strength and courage.

CHAPTER ONE

Marriage To Walt

"If Music Be The Food of Love, Play On"

*"So now Abideth Faith, Hope, Love, These Three;
but the Greatest of These is Love."*

1 Corinthians 13:13

The strains of Rachmaninoff's Concerto, Number 2 in C Minor, slowly move through the room. Its crescendos move my spirit, speak to me of peace and comfort. I carry these sounds within my heart. They never cease to swell the tears of my soul, tears I've held back so long. They speak to me of my losses, my sorrows, my joys, as the music rises and falls over and over again. The composer wrote this in a time of despair, a time when he questioned his own talent, as I question mine to put on these pages the feelings from within. Years later he was quoted as saying this piece of music helped him to take courage and have faith. This music *is* love... courage and faith follow. This is the fiftieth anniversary of his death. An appropriate time to remember...

Every man who went through the Lutheran seminary in St. Louis to train as a pastor left home at the age of fourteen to enter a prep school of his choosing. There were about nine around the country at that time, so Walter Oetting, my future husband, selected Concordia College in Fort Wayne, Indiana (a seminary prep school as well as a military school) for the beginning of his studies. This was Walt's father's home town, and his Aunt Erna still lived on the old homestead bought many years earlier by his grandfather. It was here in Fort Wayne that he made life-long friends who would later follow in his footsteps to teach at Concordia Seminary (Prof. Robert Bergt for one).

Walt had never been away from home before and at age 14 he faced a very lonely existence. His mother saved every sad letter he wrote, and there were many. She kept every letter her four children had written, even all those of mine written in later years. She was quite an historian! I've had occasion to read some of these letters recently, and they touched my heart. Walt remained there two years, but eventually his parents, who understood his need for nurturing, allowed him to return home and complete his education in the Waterloo public high school. This was the right decision for Walter. My brother-in-law, Robert Henry Brauer, still resents his own leaving home at fourteen and attending a prep school far away; the loneliness of those formative years hurts even now in his retirement. That sadness cannot be erased.

After high school, Walt attended Valparaiso University, where he was able to take all the necessary course work as well as give vent to his abiding love of theater and music. It was here at Valparaiso that he met people who would prove to be our friends for a lifetime. Walter Bauer, Edward Schroeder, Walter Keller, Walter Rast, Robert Bertram,

Robert and Richard Duesenberg, just to mention a few. Robert and Richard Duesenberg had lost their father when they were nine years old, and their mother had raised her five children successfully on a shoe string. These young boys grew up to become brilliant, highly motivated attorneys known for their integrity and drive. Their love of the great music of our masters, like J. S. Bach, cannot be exceeded.

Since Valparaiso University was not a seminary prep school like Concordia, Fort Wayne, it did not offer the requisite Greek and Latin courses. In order to go directly to the seminary from Valparaiso, Walt and a small group of other pre-theological students petitioned for these courses, which led to the hiring of Edgar Reinke in their senior year. After graduation, Walt also took Greek and Hebrew courses at the University of Iowa in Iowa City in order to qualify for the seminary.

Walt entered Concordia Seminary in the fall of 1950, a year before I entered nurses' training at Lutheran Medical Center. We did not meet each other until 1953, when I saw him sitting in the nurses' lounge waiting to pick up one of my fellow students for a date. He wore a cap -very European looking - and he usually had his head in a book. Different...sort of handsome...hmmmmm. Was there a chance I could meet him? My friend Irene had dated him a few times, and I finally got her to introduce me to him one evening as they were leaving on a date. We chatted briefly, and I remember thinking it would be nice to go out with him. I couldn't forget him...but I didn't see him again until that spring when I attended the graduation ceremony at Concordia Seminary for my brother-in-law, Wallace Misterek. This was many months after that fleeting introduction. We literally bumped into each other afterwards at the reception. We were spontaneously overjoyed to see each other - like long lost friends! We joked, laughed, teased, and kidded around that evening as if we had known each other forever. Life was suddenly all gaiety as time ceased to exist for both of us. We were truly carried away... What impressed me the most about him was his sensitivity and love for things that counted but didn't cost much. He told me that he especially loved Mozart's music, and that the initial "W" in his name stood for "Wolfgang" (it was really Wayne!). He admitted he was an incurable romantic, and that in private he liked to see himself as Mozart, the serenader of love. Like Mozart, he too was a busy and gifted man driven to create the songs of love for the one he wooed. Walt's love for the past and its music, and for the God who made both, was infectious - I fell in love with him that very night, and he with me. We both knew it, though we'd only talked together a few hours that evening, and on into the morning - we didn't part until nearly 2 a.m., with little more than a kiss to remember. No more than that - we both knew even then we would save The Real Thing for our wedding day.

We parted that morning knowing we wouldn't see each other again until the fall. He returned to Waterloo for work that summer and I returned to my studies at Lutheran Hospital. Could it be I would never see him again? I knew from past experience that men would come and go. Just maybe he'd forget me. But he started writing me that day and every day! Could it be true? My heart raced every time a letter came from him; did I dare invest myself completely in this one man I'd known just a few short hours? I responded to every letter - and they *were love* letters. Wow! I didn't know when I'd see him again, as he would be off somewhere for a year of vicarage, an internship for student pastors to give them experience out of the "Ivory Tower" and into the real world of regular people. After that he'd return to Concordia for his final year of study, and then graduation. Well, I decided, this tall, dark, handsome, and intelligent man with the glorious wavy black hair and keen wit *would* be mine! Little did I know he was thinking the same about me.

Along about mid-summer he wrote that he wanted me to meet his family and his parents, the Reverend Walter and Mrs. Edna Oetting. I took the train (I decided this man was worth the money!) and spent five days of my vacation with him. Of course the anxiety of meeting his parents just overwhelmed me. My heart actually raced the whole time I was there, if you can imagine. Relax, I said to myself. So what if his father, this highly esteemed, staunch man of the cloth, who had graduated from that same Concordia Seminary (in 1922), *was* the well-known President of the Iowa East District of the Lutheran Church-Missouri Synod, *and* also head of the largest congregation in Iowa? He was also a charter member and distinguished chairman of the board of Allen Hospital in Waterloo, Iowa. He had a wife too. Edna, like my mom, worked very hard, as all pastors' wives did. Pastors' wives took good care of the pastor and his family, keeping a low profile, but having a high interest in the needs of many in their congregation. They were not to talk too much, or too little. Their attitude and behavior was to suit the needs of many, but be friendly to all: a model wife and mother for others to emulate. About like the Queen of England, you know. Yes, parishioners had high expectations of these women. Many still keep the pastor and his wife on a pedestal today.

Walt's mother was not there that weekend - she had suddenly been called away to help her oldest daughter, Gloria, after the birth of her and Ros Jensen's first child, Paul. I was disappointed that I could not meet the head of the manse. I had heard such good things from Walt about her. His younger brother, Louis, was home from college. He was also preparing to become a pastor. (He later graduated from Concordia Seminary, then married Sharon Krahl.) Walt's teenage sister, Mary, was living at home going to high school. (She later married Norb Brummond.) Mary and I did all the cooking; neither of us was experienced but I guess we produced something edible. What a test for a future wife who had little knowledge in the kitchen! I was embarrassed, to say the least, at not being able to cook at age 21. After all, I had been away from home since I was fifteen and getting a different kind of education! But I could carry on a decent conversation, and Walt was obviously gone on me at that point, so I guess all in all I proved to be a suitable catch for him. Walt was not a man who could be stopped, regardless.

He came to St. Louis in late summer to spend several days with me before his long and lonely trip to Austin, Texas. He would teach during his nine months of vicarage. He was talking marriage right from the start! He was the boss, and I certainly was willing. Next year, he said, before he completed his last year of studies at Concordia, might be a good time to think about getting married. I would finish my training near the end of August. That would be 1954.

Walt picked me up in his old '38 Ford for Christmas of '53. We drove the 100 miles near Effingham, Illinois (Island Grove parish in the country), to meet my parents, and to get my Dad's approval for our marriage. My parents had moved from North Dakota to Illinois several years before. I was so proud to introduce him to my parents, the Reverend Walter and Mrs. Helen Leininger. My dad did not have any special titles, but he was a man of wisdom and distinction who had also graduated from Concordia Seminary in St. Louis (in 1923). My mother was a woman of great intelligence and endurance. They both had the kind of courage and strength that I hoped to have. Those years in Canada and North Dakota were their training ground - and I respected and loved them. Mom took great pride in having straight A's at

Shortridge High School in Indianapolis. She graduated with honors and went on to be *the* bookkeeper at a *fancy* store (as she called it), the Meyer Brothers Company in town.

My parents seemed to like Walt from the start. At least I sensed that, although they were not much for verbalizing their feelings. Mom was always quiet and proper around everyone. She was a good pastor's wife. She remembered being called the "Frau Pastorin" up there in Saskatchewan, Canada (where I was born). "Mrs. Pastor" did ring true for her. She had raised their five children, four girls and one boy, well. Let me just tell you a bit about my family here. My oldest sister, Dorothy, taught school for many years before marrying a preacher, Wallace Misterek, whom I mentioned earlier. They had their first child, Paul, by then. My next sister, Lois, likewise taught school and had recently married William Krenning, who was about to graduate from the same Concordia Seminary in St. Louis! I was next in line as the middle child. As the third girl, they must have been a little disappointed! If they were, I never felt a twinge of that. I ended up marrying a preacher from the same Seminary as well! The folks never gave up having a boy though. Finally their only son, Robert Walter, was born. He became a teacher and musician, later marrying Phyllis Pruitt, who had also been a teacher. Last but not least was sister Estelle, who has always been "Tudy" to everyone. She did secretarial work, and later married Larry Downing, a twenty-year military man. I am happy and proud to report that my siblings and original spouses are still together at this writing. We all had the same sense of commitment and set of values - something I feel noteworthy to say in 1994!

Back to Christmas 1953. We left my home near Effingham, Illinois, for Walt's home in Waterloo, Iowa. It was a couple of days before Christmas. This would give me some time to meet and get acquainted with his mother, this courageous woman I'd heard so much about. She was a woman of character and strength who took pride in raising her four children. Sewing was sheer joy for her. Every stitch of clothing her children wore was made by her she used to tell me. She was a gifted seamstress who made both her daughters' wedding dresses, and eventually sewed mine. My mother also sewed, but out of necessity.

I found Mother Oetting easy to talk with. We hit it off from the start, making me feel very relaxed. She cooked and baked the finest food a preacher could afford. I remember well how impressed I was with the flaming plum pudding she made for dinner on Christmas Eve!

She came from a well-known St. Louis family, the Nolkempers. She worked a few years at the Brown Shoe Company before marrying the Reverend at the age of twenty-two. Mother Oetting had only finished sixth grade, but she obviously had learned well all she needed to know. I thought she was terrific. She always made me feel good about myself, and was a ready friend who would teach me about being a pastor's wife. She was a good one, like my mother, I thought. She could "do her own thing" and yet still be submissive enough to be unnoticed, as was expected of that position in those days. Walt's dad, on the other hand, was a man of power and prestige. You would not cross or challenge him. No one did that I know about.

It was during this visit that Walt took me completely by surprise. After the Christmas Eve dinner with the family all around, he took my hand and led me into the living room. He sat me down, reached for my left hand and slipped on a beautiful diamond solitaire ring. I thought I would faint from excitement - I couldn't believe it! How could it be that I would be so lucky? This naive country girl from a small prairie town in North Dakota had come to the big city and had gotten her man; the man of her dreams, the man she deserved, for had she too not studied and worked as hard to achieve her goals as he? She was ready to become a complete woman, a wife and mother. Nursing would be something to fall back on in later years.

After that grand and unforgettable Christmas in 1953, we did not see each other until the following June. Walt came for my graduation from nurses' training at Lutheran Hospital, now called Lutheran Medical Center. What an exciting event! It was June, 1954 at Holy Cross Lutheran Church where I received my nursing pin and diploma. There were 39 of us. We could wear all white now as full-fledged nurses, prepared to work as Registered Nurses. A goal I had finally achieved! I felt like I *was* a rose truly blessed, as Walt told me in letters.

After graduation, I stayed on to complete the last requirement of floor duty just three days before we were married. It was during these ecstatic days that Mother Oetting and I selected a basic pattern for my wedding dress. She was eager to sew it, and eager to please me. She could make the dress however I wanted it, she said. We chose carefully the imported Chantilly lace for most of the dress, and added tiers of tulle and lace which cascaded down the back into a long train. She did not worry about any fittings. She was a woman of faith, so confident in her sewing that she knew it would fit. Thus I did not worry either. We did the planning of it mostly by diagrams in letters. I will never forget the day I received it in the mail. My friends and I eagerly opened the large package, my hands shaking. They helped me get into it painstakingly buttoning each tiny lace button down the back. It fit just about perfect! I was privileged to wear this dress in several bridal pageants in the years to come.

With the help of our parents we made plans for our wedding and the big day came together with nary a hitch, at least none that I can remember. It was all done at long distance, mostly by letter. Telephoning was a luxury we seldom enjoyed.

I was married to Walter Wayne Oetting on August 22, 1954 in a quiet setting out in the country I've always loved. The place was near Effingham, Illinois, called Island Grove in my Dad's church. It had the familiar parsonage, church, and cemetery. An iron fence separated it from the two-lane road which slipped silently over the fields until it vanished over the next hill on its way to town.

Ours was a lovely wedding, simple and quiet, really - made all the more special in that our fathers presided. Our closest families and friends joined us in celebrating our great fortune of finding each other. Everything about our future looked bright. Walter had finished his master's degree in Ancient and Medieval history at Washington University, alongside a Bachelor of Divinity degree at Concordia Seminary, both in St. Louis. I had completed my nurses' training. We were both ready to take on the world, and we expected to become what we wanted to be together as husband and wife.

After a quiet and secluded honeymoon at Brown County State Park in Indiana, we returned to St. Louis to settle into our first home on Oxford Avenue in the community of Maplewood. Walter continued his final year of study at Concordia Seminary, while I started a new job as an operating room nurse at Deaconess Hospital.

That first year passed quickly and happily as I worked and he studied and wrote his final Bachelor of Divinity thesis for graduation. I was thrilled to find I could even help him edit his paper; spelling was not his forte. I found that all the drills I'd done in my North Dakota small country schools really came in handy!

Walt had a deep love of the arts, especially acting, which he carried over from his high school days in Waterloo, Iowa, and later from Valparaiso University. I know he found some of his acting skills helpful in his ministerial work. Since he also loved music, especially the classics, he introduced me to some of the "finer" things in our culture. I had some exposure to the arts in my years at Dr. Martin Luther College in New Ulm, Minnesota, but I don't think I had enough time to internalize the true beauty of the classics.

Early in our marriage he handed me his copy of <u>The Story of Art</u> by E. H. Gombrich. I read it through, at first dutifully, then hungrily. When I finished I wanted more, because now I knew our lovely Art Museums were out there - for us to enjoy together.

I became aware of all the culture St. Louis offered; there was no end of places to see, things to do, great music to hear, food in some of the greatest restaurants... I loved going to our St. Louis Symphony (now internationally ranked), our unsurpassed Municipal Opera which has for seventy-five years been a summer tradition for St. Louis music lovers, our many parks, our grand theaters like the Fox, our gardens, Missouri Botanical for one, and our Zoo. In my kitchen I became addicted to Concordia's KFUO classical music radio station, as well as KMOX and their sports and talk shows. Those voices over the air will never be forgotten by any of us older folks.

Walt and I were learning what it meant to give and take as we adjusted to each other's idiosyncracies. He learned to sacrifice some of his love of solitude for time with me, while I learned to respect his need for silence and deep thought. The material things so many people think are important in their lives were absent in those years. They seemed unimportant to us. He owned an old blue '38 Ford, in which I passed my driver's license test shortly after the wedding. Somehow we managed to collect enough pieces of furniture for our efficiency apartment whose tiny kitchen and bath we shared with another man, about whom we knew little. We had a lot of books plus Walt's sizeable record collection (he *loved* collections), and our wedding gifts (toasters and irons), which enabled us to manage our efficient, though meagerly furnished, little household. Actually, I brought almost nothing material to the marriage, but what I lacked there, I more than made up for with my enthusiasm for life, my love for Walt, and my ability to keep us afloat on my $250.00 a month salary as a surgical nurse at Deaconess Hospital. (This included over-time on-call work twice a week for emergency surgeries; I usually stayed overnight in the nurses' residence to save time and gas.)

We made friends with other seminarian families, like Pfotenhauers, Underwagers, Weyermanns, Hoyers, Bergts, P. Maier, Kalins, Trinkleins, K. Thiele, just to mention a few. I still maintain contact with some through letters or Christmas cards; our shared experiences as student couples created a strong bond. I think each of these men felt they had wives who fit the job description delineated in Proverbs 31: 10-31, that they be "from the Lord." We were their treasures as wives, mistresses and mothers, whose worth was far above jewels. Strength and honor was to be ours, as we would be full of wisdom and kindness, as it says in the scriptures.

We looked forward to May of 1955 when Walt would graduate and his formal studies would be over (though I knew he would never stop studying!). After all these years of study, he would finally be qualified to serve God as a man of the cloth, a pastor to his flock.

Walt and Rose Marie
August 22, 1954

Don and Rose Marie
August 31, 1968

Walt's Ordination
St. Joseph, Michigan, 1955

Walt doing his favorite thing
1955

Graduation from Lutheran Medical
School of Nursing, 1954

Dad's 40th anniversary
in the Ministry
Leininger Family, September 1963

Three families in Rose Marie's life:
Leiningers, Oettings, and Brauers

Oetting family, June 1969

Don-Graduation from River Forest, Illinois,
1956

Brauer family
1954

Baptism of Tom and Andy
November 1957

Walt, Rose Marie and two new sons,
November 1957

Having fun typing

Andy and Tom
My two cub scouts

Tom, Greg, Andy
8 1/2, 2, 7
Cute kids!

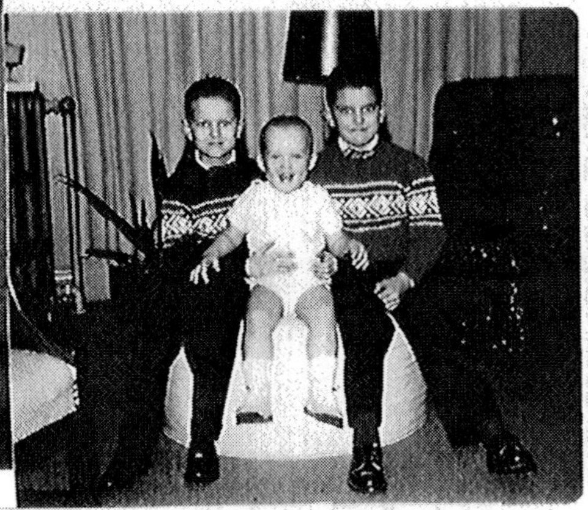

My 3 sons So loved!

CHAPTER TWO

ORDINATION
ADOPTION OF CHILDREN

"And His Gifts Were That Some
Should Be Apostles,
Some Prophets, Some Evangelists,
Some Pastors, and Teachers,
For the Perfecting of the Saints,
For the Work of the Ministry,
For Building up the Body of Christ."

Ephesians 4:11-15

Walt's graduation from the seminary was June 3, 1955 - a day we both looked forward to with the greatest excitement. His dad would have his first born son (born on his own birthday, April 25) to follow in his footsteps to serve the Lord in the ministry. How could a father be more proud and happy? His mother had nurtured, loved and cared for him so much, and he was to be what a mother in those days wanted him to be, a preacher. Besides that he was getting a good woman to be at his side. The world was ours! God had blessed us so richly. Our families were there to be with us to celebrate this mountain top experience. In First Corinthians 12 it gives the seven gifts of the Spirit that the members of the body of Christ possess. The different colored stoles a pastor wears is a reminder of these gifts. Wisdom (purple), Knowledge (red), Faith (gold), Healing (purple), Miracles (red), Prophecy (gold), Gift of Tongues (purple.) But the greatest gift of all is love - if we have not love we have nothing. (1 Cor. 13.) This gift we felt we had in fullest measure. This day was a celebration and a farewell - this was the time we said goodbye to many friends we had made. Our lives might cross somewhere - but for now there was no looking back. Our educations were complete and the future was ours to take. The friends would be moving to the far reaches of the earth - even foreign countries. Goodbyes were mixed with joy and sadness. Life *would* go on in serving the Lord through serving others. He did not say it would be easy.

Walt's first call was to serve in a mission parish in St. Joseph, Michigan. It sounded like a wonderful place as we speculated on what we imagined it would be like. Our first "real" home and congregation! Could this really be? Walt's Dad had served in the largest Lutheran congregation in Waterloo, Iowa, for most of his ministry, except for the first six years in Davenport, Iowa, where Walt was born.

Christ Lutheran in St. Joseph was a wonderful place to be, as it turned out. We were there four and a half years. It is a lovely town on Lake Michigan, a tourist town getaway retreat for Chicagoans for whom it was just a two-hour drive. The lake is so huge, and the waves so high... for a prairie girl it was like living right on the ocean. That was where we lived our first six months -in a beach house one half block from the lake. I can still hear the roar of those waves in stormy weather; the water was a bit frightening at times.

We were welcomed by kind folks, for whom our wish seemed their command. They were the "Salt of the Earth," reminiscent of my family and friends in North Dakota. On the average, they were our age or a little bit older and some had completed a higher education at Valparaiso University, like Walt, only 60 miles away. (Later, Walt would commute two days a week there to teach history.)

They had formed this little "mission" congregation out in the suburbs - a branch of the mother congregation, Trinity, in downtown St. Joseph. There was potential to reach many folks who were building new homes out on the edge of town. A large piece of land was purchased for the future combination church and school. Our house was then in the process of being built across the street. Members of the church were builders, electricians, plumbers with many talents among the men and women. They completed a home for us - modern and streamlined, a home in which neither Walt nor I would have imagined we would live.

We both had lived in large *old*, drafty homes as was typical of most parsonages in those days. This home had everything built in, including the wall oven and table top stove. What a novelty! There was even a counter extending out so we could sit on stools to eat meals if we chose not to eat in the dining room. Wall to wall hardwood floors were put in - lovely, but not easy to keep looking nice. The soil surrounding the house was all clay, with a grape vineyard on one side, and fruit trees on two other sides. These were owned by the local farmers who were generous in sharing the produce with us. Many members had large orchards, vineyards and gardens - truly a paradise for fruit and wine lovers, as we came to be. They generously shared these gifts from heaven with us and even taught me how to can or freeze the produce. My folks had taught me some things, but to do this canning on my own was a whole new ball game! Among the members I had willing teachers, and I was a willing learner. I eventually mastered the art of canning with Walt's help. We put up as many as 300 jars of produce in a year! Can you imagine that! He loved grape juice canned in 2-quart jars, which we made simply from a dear lady's recipe, whose name I don't recall.

Members of the parish invited Walt to do some "regular guy" stuff like bowling and fishing - a way to get away from the pressures of parish life. When we left St. Joseph's these sports came to an end.

When I look back on those days, I think of the peace that was ours. On the other hand, adjusting to being the pastor's wife was not easy either. I needed and wanted to feel close to our people, but the role as pastor's wife in those days and in our particular location was considered "conservative." That meant that the pastor's wife was always called "Mrs. So and So." I was not called by my first name by our members - even by those who were my age. I thought that a bit strange, but Walt said that was "proper" for pastors' wives. Both our mothers were generally called "Mrs." and somehow that did not seem strange, but for me, it did. I longed for a closeness among my peers, but that was frowned upon. I did what was considered the right and proper thing at all times, just as our mothers had. I would not have considered "breaking out of the mold." I was a product of my *genes and* my *environment*. The longer I live the more I feel sure of that. They work together.

I did join the local Valparaiso University Guild, which was made up generally of Trinity members. I developed a close bond with these women. However, even though these women called me by my first name, I always maintained my "pastor's wife" status - no wavering.

My dear friend then and yet today was the other pastor's wife, Elsa Zschoche, who was from the "big" church, Trinity. She still is the ultimate in "pastor's wife" perfection. I tried to model her behavior. We got along famously. She, being about 20 years my senior, took me under her wing and was like a mother to me. I could tell her some of the feelings and fears I had, and she would always understand.

How Elsa could work! The big, old house in town kept her cleaning, scrubbing and wiping from morning to night. When a special occasion was coming up, she would be wiping the rain drops off the windows at the very last minute! She used rumpled newspapers. Clever idea, I thought. I still use them on our cars to this day. She had three young daughters, Claire Ann, Anita, and Elaine, whom she tenderly cared for and taught how to keep a perfect house - I wondered if she ever slept...

Her Martin, whom she loved dearly, was the illustrious pastor at the "big church." Now Martin Zschoche was a man who loved life, God, people, and sports (not necessarily in that order). He, too, like my kind Uncle Richard Torgler, a pastor at Emmaus in St. Louis, liked to joke around. (I was a student nurse when we became well acquainted.) He knew more jokes and could tell one after another - always of the clean variety, I might add. (At least, that was in front of us women.) He was a joy to be around!

Martin was good for Walt who tended to be more serious now that he was out in the ministry. Walt tended to get headaches, but Martin's humor eased the pressures of life as a busy pastor. We developed a very close bond with Martin and Elsa, one I cherish in my memory. Elsa has been widowed twice since then.

Walt believed in letting the congregation do the leading, contrary to many pastors in those days. After all, he had a very upscale, intelligent membership, which included many persons highly qualified to do any job. He was there as their teacher and Shepherd to guide them along the way spiritually.

The congregation had taken on a large building program. There was a large school, where we held services in the gym. The membership gradually increased as the school opened. More and more people were marrying and building homes in the suburbs of St. Joseph. Eventually they would build a church attached to the school, but for now the school with a gym for the children to play was of utmost importance. A Christian education in a parochial school was foremost in helping parents "bring up their children in the nurture and admonition of the Lord."

Most mothers stayed home and took care of the little ones, canned, cooked and cleaned and took tender care to run a smooth household. As they used to say in German, "Kinder, Küche, und Kirche" (children, kitchen, and church) was the role of the woman. Ultimately, what more important thing was there, or as a matter of fact, is there, if you have babies? It is a full-time job and God gave us little ones to nurture and love.

Meanwhile, Walt was receiving phone calls from both his alma maters, Valparaiso University and the St. Louis Seminary to come back to teach. At first he would not consider a change. He was finding the parish and its people to be an enjoyable and secure way of life. Why go back to the big hectic city? So we settled into the pleasant life in St. Joseph, Michigan, for four and a half years.

Michigan had a lot of snow and cold weather. It seemed we had winters like my old North Dakota, where I was raised. One bad winter in Michigan we had three accidents with our only car, and no time in between for repairs! The one accident I will never forget. The embarrassment of colliding with the local doctor one icy day was an unforgettable experience! Not the best of circumstances to get acquainted, but that was the beginning of a friendship.

Our dear friend, Martin, had so many accidents that year no company would insure him! One of his retired members drove him everywhere after he was hit by a slow-moving train. That was the final straw! He was dragged by the train for quite a distance, but came out with hardly a scratch. God was always with these preachers it seems. How well I remember my Dad's "heavy foot" with some narrow escapes from the jaws of death!

Life was pretty routine after a while. In the back of our minds were babies. The desire to have a little one in our midst to love and care for grew stronger. I had a spontaneous abortion (6 weeks along) the first year we were in St. Joseph. Even though it saddened me, I was at least happy I *could* get pregnant. During nurses' training the surgeon who did my appendectomy told me my ovaries were full of cysts, so I'd better not wait long before having children.

I kept myself busy in the meantime, pursuing other avenues to improve myself, in addition to the tasks as a pastor's wife. I took several courses at the local high school, first enrolling in an evening Woodworking course. With great pride and much labor, I made a cabinet to house our large collection of records. (It is still used in our living room today.) My weakness for beautiful clothes was remedied by taking a tailoring course, where I made myself a soft wool suit. I wore it for many years, and continued to sew many clothes which I could not have afforded to buy.

Well, I wasn't getting pregnant, and I loved babies. I had shelved nursing, as it was frowned upon in our area for a pastor's wife to have employment outside the home. I thought it would be a joy to offer foster care for babies. It would fill a void in my life, and help some little ones as well. So I checked with our local agency on fostering babies. It was no time at all and I had two little girls to care for: Julie Ann and Stacey Beth. They were absolutely precious. I could not believe being in full charge of two one-month-old babies day and night. What a fun challenge! Their care seemed to come naturally for me. I had nursery experience in nurses' training; however, my schedule had to change. I slept when they slept, and was awake when they were awake.

Walt went along with this plan of caring for these babies, but I'm not so sure he liked the idea as much as I did. I got in a routine of holding one and propping the other one's bottle - having them take turns so they both received closeness and nurturing. I had a bassinet that carried them both. They were quite the center of attention everywhere I went! I was beginning to love these little ones, who were a real joy. It ended all too soon, however. Within six weeks a suitable match was made, and they were adopted by a couple in Michigan. Deep down I had hoped to adopt them, but we had not even applied for adoption. True as it was, it was a terribly sad day when the social worker came and picked up those two precious babies. I was not permitted to meet the lucky new parents. I never saw these little angels again. It was not wise to pursue any further attachment, they said.

Later they asked if we would be interested in fostering three brothers - ages one, three and five. "Sure," I said. I felt pretty competent in child rearing at that point. One week later, I had two of the brothers visit with me for half a day. Their names I have changed to protect their privacy. These two little guys, Thomas, aged three, and Andrew, one and a half, looked like little waifs in dire need of some loving. Not a smile was to be seen. Their hair was long, (for those days) and their fingernails were bitten down to the quick. *Active* was hardly the word for their behavior! Andy was an amazing phenomenon! He was so quick that he would hit his big brown head on both sides of the doorway as he went dashing through! Up and down the stairs he went, investigating everything for a moment and then racing on to something else. He sat on my lap in the rocker in a rare moment of tiredness and we rocked and rocked. Absolutely his favorite thing to do! At first he would not sit and let me rock him no matter how tired, but later he succumbed.

Tommy, who had long blonde hair, had already internalized some of his anxiety. He took to sitting and biting his fingernails. He was more distant and seemed almost grown up before his time. But wasn't he only three, I asked myself?

Both boys said little, but observed everything with their huge, sad, beautiful brown eyes. My heart was taken by their apparent need for love. I certainly felt I had enough love to give. Little did I know it could never be enough, and love not totally accepted by them. I learned later from the social worker that these children had been physically and emotionally neglected by their parents! They had suffered so long - their life had been an arid desert devoid of nurturing. Maybe their fate was already sealed within their anxious little bodies.

My heart and soul went out to them that day, so pathetic was their plight. A month later they were literally handed to us to keep. I couldn't turn them away. It must be God's will, I said to myself. Walt was not as taken by these children. His life was very busy and he could not consider sharing a lot more of his time. However, if I wanted to share my life in bringing up these little boys, that was pretty much up to me, he said.

A week after their visit, the social worker brought over the third brother, a five year old, along with Tommy and Andy. Now this little guy, John, I'll call him, had the whole world already on his shoulders. He *knew* and *remembered* no one *really* caring for *him*. He seemed angry and had transferred his anxiety and fear into teasing. The mental anguish could be seen in his eyes. Oh, God, I could not care for him too, I said to Walt. What could I do? I was only one person. These three boys, though brothers, did not appear to know or care for one another. They each needed so many arms to enfold them. There was not enough love to pass around to *three* boys starved for love...How sad to separate brothers, I thought. What kind of mother could give up her beautiful children? My consolation was that they had been separated already by being placed in different foster homes for over a year. The two oldest had been in numerous foster homes, I was told. We could at least help bring two together and give them a permanent home, possibly. However, it did not help the guilty feeling I kept for many years at not taking the third child.

The social worker informed us that their parents had a "common law" relationship and did not wish to marry. Their biological father came home ad lib, got his woman pregnant, and was on his way again. The children had become wards of the court in the State of Michigan, because the mother would not take care of them either. How my heart bleeds for the things children have to suffer at the whims of their so-called parents!

It was November of 1957 that Tommy and Andy, who "had dropped from heaven," came to live with us. I was sure we could all *learn* to truly love each other even if we did not feel it yet. We prayed constantly for it. At least they had a "Mommy and Daddy," as Tommy called us from the very start. Thomas's real name was not changed, but we did give him a new middle name, Walter. Since he was our eldest, he would be privileged to have that name. He would carry the name of "Walter" for his father and both grandfathers. Walt wanted to change our youngest boy's name to Andrew Louis (after Walt's brother). The social worker did not seem concerned and did not discourage it. I would not do it today, but this was 1957. Who was concerned then for the emotional effects this could have on a child? Little was talked about that! They would survive, wouldn't they? We were a suitable home with two emotionally healthy people. That is all they were looking for in parents. Andy learned slowly to call us "Mommy and Daddy" - he proceeded with a little more caution.

Well, did those two new sons of ours get attention! It must have been quite shocking to them to see how the members of our church opened their arms to love them. The boys did respond well to a lot of attention, and were very active! I was not exactly used to all the activity and neither was Walt. We were learning to adjust slowly to the vigor and alacrity of daily living

One Sunday afternoon we were surprised with a *huge* shower of clothes and toys for Tommy and Andy. I actually counted 60 pieces of clothing of various sizes - enough to last for a few years. It was overwhelming! Our members knew how much it would cost us to clothe them, and how little we had on a preacher's salary! These kind-hearted folks gave freely of their hearts and pocketbooks. Such an outpouring of love we had never seen before! To this day, I hold a special place in my heart for the many friends in St. Joseph, Michigan.

Tommy and Andy were quite the performers and when folks would come over they would perform for them. Tommy especially wasn't shy. Andy would just follow what Tommy would do - sometimes that was good and sometimes bad. Quite typical of two little boys.

One day not long after they came to be our children, Tommy took Andy's hand, and off they went exploring the neighborhood. I was in the house canning vegetables when I noticed they were gone. We were frantically looking for them for two hours, before we alerted the police, and finally located them! Back through the orchard they had walked, and had ended up at someone's back door - lost! *That* was the beginning of Tommy's new pattern of enjoying an occasional disappearance. That became his favorite way to get attention for many years to come. Andy had his brother to follow and model his behavior.

Andy loved the to and fro of rocking, whether it was in a rocking chair, his rocking horse, or in his bed - he would rock hard and long, his big, brown eyes serious and intent. Never will I forget those sad eyes...I always figured he must have been left in his crib alone for *hours* as an infant, because he continuously rocked back and forth. He could move any piece of furniture across the room with his rocking! That was the only way he could go to sleep. That kept us from sleeping. Our bedroom was under theirs. We finally put Andy in a regular solid bed and that helped a lot. We gradually got used to the rocking sound, but not without some sleepless nights.

Tommy found his niche in being Mommy's little helper with Andy. He hustled for diapers and would also sit with Andy in the bathroom when I was trying to train him. A new adventure for me as well!

The new speed of life was not easy for any of us, but we gradually were learning to adjust to one another. Andy's refusal to sit on Walt's lap was a blow to him. Andy did not trust this big man who was supposed to be his father. He was Mommy's boy only. Tommy was eager for our attention, but I never felt it was enough for him. It was hard to make up for his first three years. There just wasn't enough time to catch up. Now he shared attention with his younger brother, who needed more of my time. Life just was not fair, was it?

We were not strangers to adoption. Earlier, my sister, Lois, and her husband, Bill, had adopted their oldest child as a baby. They went through a private agency in Texas and ended up paying thousands of dollars for their little one. Also later, my sister, Tudy (Estelle), and her husband, Larry, adopted two boys when they were babies. But we all lived so far apart. Maybe it would have been helpful for these adopted children to know their cousins who were also adopted. Possibly some further bonding would have taken place, but that did not happen. Distance kept us many miles apart.

Our families opened their arms to welcome Tommy and Andy on their Baptismal Day. They gathered in St. Joseph for this moving and memorable time. Thinking back to that day over thirty-five years ago, those memories of laughter and tears seem like yesterday. I vividly remember the tears I cried for these little guys that day. They came probably from joy, mixed with sadness for their deprived past, and fear for their future. God had taken care of them thus far, and we were sure He would continue to guide us in caring for His children. My life took on a deeper meaning as a mother of two. I was happy taking care of my husband and family. They were my pride and priority.

CHAPTER THREE

BACK TO CONCORDIA SEMINARY
BIRTH OF OUR BABY, GREGORY
THE 1960'S EVOLVING

"Oh Sing to the Lord a New Song for
He Has Done Marvelous Things!"

Psalm 98:1

Life was getting much busier for Walt and me. Caring for our two new sons was a lot for me to handle with the responsibilities of a pastor's wife as well. Just being present and doing what was expected, besides maintaining "perfection," took a lot of my energy. Our mothers had done it. We were as "perfect" as preacher's kids could be (P.K's as we were called).

Besides being a pastor of our growing church, Walt was again asked to teach History part-time at Valparaiso University in Indiana. His favorite subject! He could not resist. Two afternoons a week he jumped into the world of academics. Sometimes we all went along just to communicate with each other on the sixty-mile drive. We were developing friendships with several of the professors' families there. They too were having babies. We felt a common bond, and a freedom of expression. Walter and Gloria Keller are still there as I write these pages. They are very dear people whom I seldom see, but we still write at Christmas. Robert and Thelda Bertram are now in St. Louis after his having taught at Valparaiso University and at Concordia Seminary. He is retired from Lutheran School of Theology at Chicago (LSTC) and continues to teach Biblical and Historical Education courses at various universities as well as "Crossings" with Ed and Marie Schroeder - other dear friends from Valparaiso University and Concordia Seminary days. The best man for our wedding, Walt Rast and his Susie, as well as Richard Baepler, have been at Valparaiso for many years. These friends are "institutions" in their own right (bulwarks of that beloved University). Herta and Walt Bauer, who was the son of Valparaiso's Dean, were very close friends of Walt. We still keep in touch. I knew there were a lot of Walts in my life, but until this writing, I had not been impressed with the number! Maybe there will be another Walt who will come along in the next generation to carry on that memory...

Dr. O. P. Kretzmann was the austere President of Valparaiso University during the 50's and 60's. He had a power and charisma that built that university into one of the best institutions of higher education. He had an aura about him which endeared him to people all over the country. This gentleman tried hard to convince Walt to become a full-time teacher on his faculty. I recall the contacts and conversations, but Walt liked the parish life and the people. He was content for now to keep his contact with teaching on a part-time basis.

The pressure was on when he received communications culminating in a "call" (a written formal request) from Concordia Seminary in 1958. Dr. Alfred Fuerbringer, President of the Seminary, wanted him to return to St. Louis to teach for him. Obviously, they had heard of Valparaiso's desire to have him, and they were not going to lose out. They wanted this bright scholar on *their* teaching staff. Now I realize this sounds like bragging, but I have to say to you, dear readers, that he was. The evidence was there.

Well, Walt was in a dilemma. He shared this with me and we prayed about it. He loved where he was, and doing what he was doing for the present. Why change all that? He was not ready for a big move. This was not yet the time, so he returned their call.

The summer of 1959 he received a second "call" from Concordia Seminary to teach Historical Theology. Time had passed. He had been a parish pastor for over four years in St. Joseph, Michigan. He had the necessary parish experience to become a teacher who had learned first hand. He had been taught by people who cared. After much prayer and deliberation, Walt decided to make the change. Obviously, the Seminary really needed and wanted *him* specifically or they would not have extended a second call to him.

We could not come for the fall semester, but would the second semester with an arrival in November be satisfactory? Both sides agreed. Walt was ready to pursue a career in teaching for which he had so diligently prepared. This was agreeable to me. The prospect was exciting! I was ready for a change out of the "fish bowl" (a common term for the life of the pastor and his family, even possibly to this day). I looked forward to closer relationships with people, even though we had many close ties in St. Joseph.

It was not easy to say our goodbyes. Life had been pleasant, and these people were very dear. Who knows when we would see them again? It was considered poor practice to return frequently to your former parish to visit. We would do whatever was recommended and taught. That was considered easier on the adjustment of a new pastor to a parish. We did not return but a few times in the years to come.

I recall the wonderful farewell they gave for us. I remember even more vividly the tears that flowed, and flow even now as I write. Our faithful Choir, directed by Earl Totzke, sang "The Lord Bless You and

Keep You." They sent us off with their prayers and many gifts. The Rohn, Schultz, Ziebart, Totzke, Kasswurm, Staude, Schaus families and many more names and faces would remain indelible in our minds. Their images are called up from my memory many times... loving thoughts of wonderful people.

We arrived in St. Louis late in November, 1959, and moved into a second floor 2-bedroom apartment owned by the Seminary. It was on San Bonita, next door to the Seminary. The five rooms were enough space for *our modest furnishings*. We would be there just a year and a half, and figured we could adjust to smaller quarters.

Below us lived Professor Philip Schroeder and his beloved wife Hattie. Such dear people! We looked to them as parent figures. "Daddy Phil," as we affectionately called him, also taught Historical Theology and enjoyed this fatherly role (they never had children). They had been married fewer years than we. Phil and Hattie were the kind of people who only mentioned in passing that Tommy and Andy's active little feet above them bothered them at all! We had many an evening glass of wine with them from the vineyards of members in St. Joseph!

Early in December, Walt was installed at Concordia Seminary along with Donald Deffner. He and Corinne had left the lovely cool Berkeley area of California, as we had left cold Michigan for the heat of St. Louis. That alone was a shock for all of us! We would not find out until the following summer that *one* 12" x 12" noisy fan would not cool an apartment... I recall with embarrassment when friends from St. Joseph came to visit. It was so hot they stayed a very short time - never to return! I am happy to report we did have a *large* window air-conditioner in the *large* home we moved into on Alamo Avenue later on. Few folks had central air even in humid St. Louis at that time. Unbelievable, isn't it? The academic atmosphere was our "cup of tea"! We loved it! The other professors with their families lived so close. We would stop by frequently to visit on an evening stroll with our sons. We settled in to these lovely surroundings and life became a little more relaxed. We had none of the pressures of a pastor and his family in the parish. That was behind us forever. Walt and I had more time to spend with Tommy and Andy, which we felt was so important for their self esteem. They attended Bethel Lutheran School where they had a wonderful start to their years of education. Dorothy Hoyer was an absolutely magnificent teacher to start with as their kindergarten teacher. We did so many family things like bicycling, ice skating, playing games, wrestling, playing ball - these were such happy times for us.

Walt was in his glory teaching Historical Theology. His education and background at Washington University in Ancient and Medieval History provided him with the perfect setting to teach. History and Theology played a fine tune in the scheme of things.

Gilbert Thiele, Head of Historical Theology, looked to Walt to write the syllabus for that department. That was a big job every summer. Also he had as many as 100 students enrolled in his seminar classes, a real opportunity for a blossoming professor! Some of these classes were the first ever to be tape-recorded at the Seminary -- quite a compliment to a young professor.

Even now, names of Walt's colleagues stand out like beacons in my mind's eye... Thiele, Krentz, Mayer, Breimeier, Scharlemann, Sauer, Caemmerer, Piepkorn, Hoyer, Danker, just to name a few. Meyer, Repp, Franszmann, Wuerffel, Bartling, Wunderlich, Bowman, Lueker, Coiner, Vincent, Schuller, Preus, Jones, Pederson, Pfitzer, Suelflow... Most of these men had taught Walt as a student. Now they were his colleagues.

Discourse between the professors was so important to Walt. He loved the open communication and exchange of ideas. Guests were frequent in our home. Lively discussions on history, religion, politics, and philosophy were the order of the day. Walt held the honor of being the youngest professor there when we arrived on campus. Almost all the men were familiar to him. They had taught him four and one half years earlier. Had they not taught him well? This is why they wanted him to be a part of the education of our future ministers in the Lutheran Church.

As the next four years unfolded many new men came to teach, names still so familiar to many in the church at large or on campuses yet today: Conrad, Bergt, Bohlmann (who later became President of the Lutheran Church-Missouri Synod), Volz, Kalin, Graesser, Michael, Wegner, Zeitler, Habel, Klann, Grunow, Johnstone. They came while we were there from all over the country. What an exciting time! The Elder Statesmen like Spitz, Bretscher, Rehwinkel, Buszin, Guebert, Sohn, Roehrs were cutting back their course load and the newer men came to take their places. They were expanding the departments as the Seminary grew. Other professors like J. T. Mueller, and Walter A. Maier still pop into my mind these many years later. Dr. Maier was the internationally renowned "Lutheran Hour" speaker over KFUO radio for many years.

Times were changing... We were becoming a large, but happy family. During this time, I was hoping and praying we would be able to have a baby. I needed a more fulfilled feeling as a mother. Since I had lost a baby in 1955, I still had not become pregnant. Margaret Thiele, Gil's wife, suggested I go to her doctor, Norman Muschany. A number of seminary wives who were also his patients said he was a very kind person, and he did not charge the clergy!

I had my first appointment with him in April 1960. (Note of interest: I had my last appointment 29 years later on June 1989 when Dr. Muschany retired.) He put me at ease from the start. I felt comfortable and confident with this man. I had been to a gynecologist in St. Joseph numerous times, but with little encouragement. Dr. Muschany assured me that with this more relaxed atmosphere I was living in, he was confident I could get pregnant. I need just take my temperature reading every morning, he added, to take advantage of my fertility cycle and I'd get pregnant. Well, I was not quite as optimistic as he.

One month later I returned for an office visit. I showed him my temperature graph and he declared happily, "Rose, it looks like you are pregnant"! I could not believe it! I had never heard such welcome words. At long last we were going to have a baby of our very own! I was "a Rose truly blessed" as Walt used to tell me.

We would not tell anyone about our terrific news for at least three months, we decided. The fear of losing another baby was still present, so Walt and I kept this wonderful, incredible joy to ourselves. We felt like shouting the news from the housetops! We could not thank God enough for our special blessing. I suspect I walked around with a smile on my face, even with a few bouts of nausea!

After the first three months I felt tip-top, and we spread the news of my being "with child" with great exuberance! Tommy and Andy were not so sure how they felt. They may have been a bit worried about competition for my attention. Our family rejoiced with us at such great news of our expected baby - a gift straight from heaven, we were sure.

That fall, during all this excitement, John F. Kennedy was elected President of the United States. We had our first Roman Catholic, young, handsome and ambitious man as head of our country. He was a controversial figure because of his religion and youth. I am proud to say, however, we were among the few on campus who voted for him.

Andy and Tommy would soon have a baby brother or sister. We would not know ahead of time if the baby was a boy or a girl. In 1960 there were no ultrasounds to give you this information. I am not so sure that we wanted to know in advance, for then the mystery would be lost.

I never felt so happy and so healthy. My life was truly blessed. The months of expectation went by all too quickly. We shopped at the second-hand furniture store and picked up a nice crib and large double chest of drawers, inexpensively. I painted it pale blue and added large decals. They were beautiful! I read "Dr. Spock" from cover to cover! I did have some fears about the delivery and about how I could handle all the responsibility, but I never was worried about having a healthy baby -I was taking good care of myself. I did not smoke, take medicine except for vitamins, or drink coffee or alcohol (to speak of). Our mothers and families did not overdo much of anything in those years! It was just not acceptable behavior for mothers in their child-bearing years. That philosophy is again gaining popularity.

Our joy was fulfilled and our prayers were answered on February 4, 1961, when our dear son, Gregory, was born. I was 29, Walt was 31 and we were ready to have and love a tiny baby. I had awakened at 3:00 A.M. with labor pains that morning, and with great anticipation called Dr. Muschany. Walt grabbed the packed suitcase and helped me to the car. We arrived safely at St. Luke's Hospital, located on Delmar Boulevard at that time. After some difficulties, which I will not reiterate, our baby was born at 4:35 P.M. that afternoon. He was 7 pounds, 9 ounces, and 20 1/2 inches of pure love, a long-awaited arrival. Praise God! I was not awake when he was born, but I can imagine Dr. Muschany and the nurse's joy to welcome our little boy into the world. Fathers were not allowed in the labor or delivery rooms, so Walt missed this great moment. That did not dampen our excitement of welcoming this "Angel from Heaven" as I will call him.

We had discussed names, but nothing decisive, since we had not known the sex of the baby. We decided on Gregory. Walt had naturally selected names from ancient men of respect and greatness: Gregory Thaumaturgus was the most famous missionary in the early church's history, because he healed those people who were "possessed with demons and disease." (He would talk to them about the Gospel, advise them about their troubles, and discuss various religious problems with them.) Gregory's middle name came from *Martin* Luther, the reformer, and Reverend *Martin* Zschoche, our dear friend.

And so it was, Gregory Martin Oetting entered his first home at 6463 San Bonita Avenue five days after delivery. His two brothers were cautious, but eager to view this new little brother, this one who was to compete for their attention and love in the years to come.

Mother Oetting and my mother came to help out after I came home from the hospital. They alternated in two-week periods. This was common practice. With the adjustment to a new baby, their maternal assistance was seen as a necessity -- an idea I agree with to this day. Caring for a newborn does not necessarily come naturally, as some may think. Our well-seasoned mothers seemed to know the important things we didn't learn in books.

He was baptized a Child of God by his father three weeks later on February 26, in the little Resurrection Lutheran Church. (This was before they built their lovely edifice.) Walt was assisting Pastor George Sommermeyer there, just to keep in touch with parish life.

One of Gregory's godparents was Bob Duesenberg, Walt's old friend from Valparaiso University days who had become very close to both of us. St. Louis was home to him as well. He was a regular at our dinner table, always bringing a bottle of the best wine or Schnapps to enhance the occasion. At age 31 Bob was still looking for a life-long companion to marry, but none had fit his stiff qualifications. We would introduce the perfect woman to him a couple of years later.

Corinne Deffner was one of Gregory's godmothers. Her husband, Dr. Donald Deffner, came on campus to teach when Walt did, as I said earlier. We had a common bond, and felt close to them in all this newness. My dear sister, Lois Krenning, was his other godmother. You couldn't have too many godparents in those days, I suppose. At least in our family it was appropriate to have three such sponsors.

There were plenty of family, friends and colleagues to rejoice with us at a dinner celebration on Gregory's Baptismal Day, a most special day in a newborn baby's life. Our Gregory became a Child of God in grand style.

After the first three weeks Gregory was weaned to the bottle, which gave him less stomach pain than mother's milk. We were both at last on a better and longer sleeping schedule.

In the months when we were preparing for our baby, we were also preparing to move into a Seminary-owned home. We were growing out of our apartment and needed space for our expanding family. Soon we would not have Hattie and Phil Schroeder below us for companionship. How I would come to miss their closeness!

The Seminary custodians were painting the entire house inside. We decided that everything from top to bottom would be ivory. The carpeting and floors were cleaned. We had purchased the lovely wall-to-wall mauve carpeting from the former professor, who recently retired to Texas. This home had spacious, airy rooms which gave one a very bright and open feeling. I thought it was heaven for us to be moving to this beautiful place, and only four blocks from the Seminary! I remember well that joy. Neither of us had ever lived in such a lovely place. Tommy and Andy would run through the huge house and investigate every corner - joy was theirs as well!

So, the spring of 1961 we moved into our little mansion at 6236 Alamo, with lots of assistance from colleagues and students. Our few furnishings almost got lost in those large rooms! On a professor's salary of around $6,000 that year (1961), we did not have extra money to buy new things. We made do, and even though that beautiful dining room with the crystal chandelier needed a lovely table and chairs to serve a lot of people in elegant style, we couldn't afford one. It had to be the wrought iron table with the formica top which could serve eight in a pinch. Food was served without china, crystal and silver, but with pottery, glass and stainless steel (all nice and necessary gifts from our wedding). The Melmac dishes were for every day. We entertained frequently in our modest, simple style.

It's strange when I look back on those days. We had so little - and yet so much. I was satisfied. Yet, I did wish I could entertain more elegantly. I always loved people, and we had a lot of "company" in and out of town.

We did not have central air conditioning. It was a luxury to own a large window unit which was installed in the dining room. With the help of fans, it was amazing how one could *almost* cool an entire house! We had four large bedrooms on the second floor. Walt used one for his office (called a "study" in those days, at least by preachers). By this time he had gathered over 500 books from second-hand purchases. Many were in his office at the Seminary, but others covered an entire wall of shelves in this study. His large oak desk and chair were given to him by friends in St. Joseph. Walt now had his place to go at home where it was quiet.

The kitchen was small, but we could still eat there. It was manageable - we could expand onto the back porch on a spring day. It was lovely, overlooking the small back yard with an old apple tree still providing fruit, although a bit wormy. I baked many an apple pie with the help of my Mom and Dad, who drove in from the country to assist me in every need.

I was not doing much canning anymore. Here there were no Michigan farmers to give us food, but on occasion we would buy a bushel of produce at one of the downtown markets and "put it up." We would purchase a quarter or a half of beef at some big sale out in the country, and put it in the deep freeze, so we would have plenty of meat to eat. Walt inherited the "meat and potatoes" taste from his father. Our Gregory has followed in their footsteps with the same propensity for simple food.

Walt was contacted by Concordia Publishing House in 1962 to begin the "Church in History" series of books. This first book would be the beginning of a history of the Church during the period from 90 to 250 A.D. It was to be written in an easy-to-read style. Youth to old age were to comprehend and use. Quite an undertaking for even a scholar who was well read! He was willing, even though it extended his working hours. It became a constant pressure to write in his spare time.

Friends often said, with a hint of irritation, that "Walt always had his nose in a book." That was true. He was always carrying one, and whatever room he entered in anyone's home, the first thing he would do was pick up and peruse any reading material lying around. He was naturally always looking for ideas for teaching or writing material.

Our close friend and symphony companion, Bob Duesenberg, asked if I knew of some single women with whom I could "fix him up." Walt and I took this seriously. We figured he needed a good woman to help take care of him. He was already 33. After several "no takes" we invited Bob to a Parent Teachers social evening at Bethel Lutheran Church, where Andy and Tommy attended school. It was a festive evening of food and fun. I knew a friend was coming in whom he might have interest, I added. Well, that particular woman did not show up, but there was someone even better! My old friend from North Dakota, Lorraine Hall, was there. She was singing in a quartet that was part of the program that evening. It was a spontaneous move on my part, which is the way I am. I took Lori by the hand, and we walked toward Bob and Walt sitting together at one of the tables. I eagerly made introductions, and then stepped back to discern their interaction. I never dreamed of the outcome. In that moment I brought two lives together. It was a "take." Walt and I just knew it, as we observed this match together. We were excited for them. I tease them to this day on how we did not see them again for months! They disappeared off the face of the earth - or so it seemed. Six months later, they announced their engagement with plans to be married in August (1963). What sensational news! How elated we were to bring them together.

Our family traveled back to North Dakota for this very important marriage of two of our best and oldest friends. Walt performed the ceremony for Bob and Lori. What a lovely wedding it was out there in that little country church in Deep River, North Dakota. That was where my Dad had baptized Lori 25 years earlier...

My youngest sister Estelle came to live with us, while her husband Larry was in the navy. We had the space and could get her a job at the Seminary. She was a big help to me as well. With three growing sons, a busy husband, and a large house which I was particular about, I welcomed the extra help and company. She was good with the boys too.

I also wanted to get back into nursing part-time to keep up my skills. How could I do this? Well, eventually Walt agreed to hire a woman to baby-sit once a week. He felt not only that I needed the additional help if I were to go back into nursing, but it would provide a part-time job for someone who needed work. I liked that idea as well.

So, in the spring of 1963 I returned to nursing for just one day a week. I worked at St. Luke's Hospital on Delmar (where Greg had been born). We hired a wonderful woman who took care of Gregory, cleaned, washed and did some cooking on the day I worked. My life seemed more balanced. I felt like it freed me to get involved in more things with the boys at school. I took Gregory with me most everywhere.

Later I expanded my interest in the fine arts. The French language was an interest I pursued at Clayton High School in their night courses. Subsequently, I took evening courses at Washington University - just for my own enrichment, concentrating on French and Literature. I even branched out into Anthropology to satisfy my curiosity. I was enjoying my new knowledge and the confidence it gave me. In retrospect, I could have concentrated on an advanced degree in nursing, but I was an idealist in those days. I wanted to learn about the fine arts. I figured I would retire from nursing after my children were through college anyway. Tudy took care of the boys on the evenings I went to school. She and I still talk today about how we would rock and sing to Gregory as a baby. We give Tudy the credit for teaching Gregory to love Coca Cola. She would sip and give him a sip while rocking and singing love songs!

I believed strongly in a long bedtime with stories for all three of the boys. After story time was prayer time. Then they were tucked in with kisses. This was our very special and important time for family closeness. We did this for many years. I pray they will remember and do the same with their families. The rocking chair is an important symbol for me and we had several. No home should be without one. It meant time out for us to love, relax and share stories. This time for closeness was also the building of good feelings toward each one of us.

As a nurse, I was called upon to volunteer my services when someone on campus needed my help. The one case in particular I remember with particular sadness. He was a young colleague of Walt's, Henry Reimann. Hank was in his early forties, when he had an aneurysm (broken blood vessel) in the brain. The neurosurgeons attempted to repair it without success. He ended up on a respirator in need of nurses around the clock to care for him. I recall my terrible feelings of sadness, and questions I had regarding my own strength. Could I care for this man with whom we were so close? How could I hold up emotionally for the family? I was afraid, but Walt in his convincing way told me I could do it. I would be able to handle it, because God would provide the strength. I do not recall how many days we nurse friends worked to help out this family, but to no avail. Hank eventually died. He left a wife and six children. How sad! His untimely death was the second one on campus in recent years. A few years earlier, a young professor had quite suddenly died of appendicitis. Their deaths were the beginning of a number of traumatic events which shook the whole Seminary, the Lutheran community, and the whole country.

We had taken for granted life would always be the same. Television depicted women's roles to be like "Ozzie and Harriet." We had a happy life with middle class values. The scenario goes like this: We worked hard; mother stayed at home (for the most part) and father earned the money to support his family: he was the "bread winner." We each had our "role" and "place" in life. Women usually took the domestic sciences if they went to college. Before getting married they generally were teachers, nurses, stewardesses, or secretaries. A child was to be *seen* and *not heard*. You obeyed your authority figures and did not ask questions. Emotions were to be controlled. One did not talk back or explain his or her side of a situation. Crying was not done often (except when spanked). Men never cried openly for fear of being thought of as unmasculine. Women for the most part cried alone in the privacy of their homes, and at funerals quietly, if necessary. That was "proper." A lot of tears was a sign of not being able to control oneself. It could even be construed as lacking faith in God. After all, God does take good care of us, so why cry over life's happenings? Honesty and integrity were assumed by most. Rules were talked about and followed without questioning the authority from which they came. This simple and uncomplicated way of life would change rapidly in the turbulent years that followed.

Our pride and joy!
Gregory

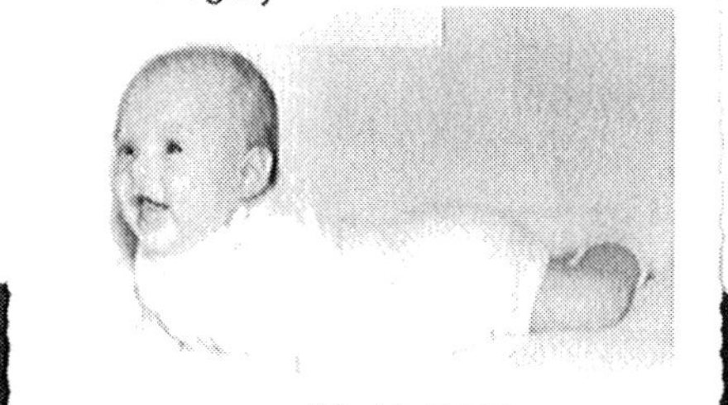

Birthdate:
February 4, 1961

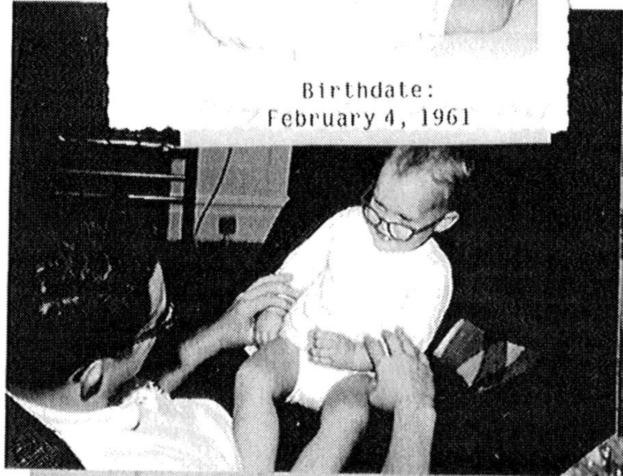

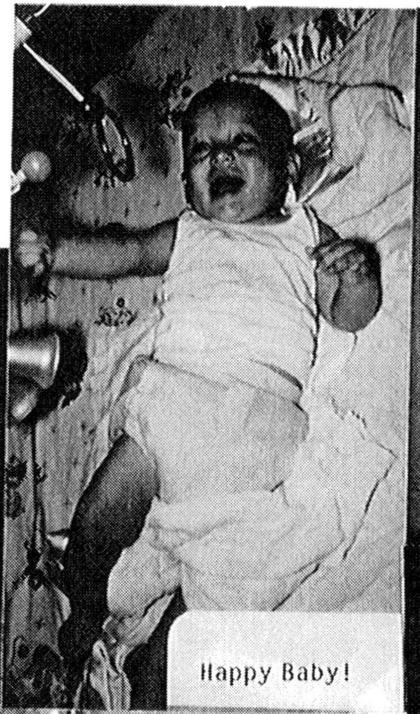

Happy Baby!

So loved!

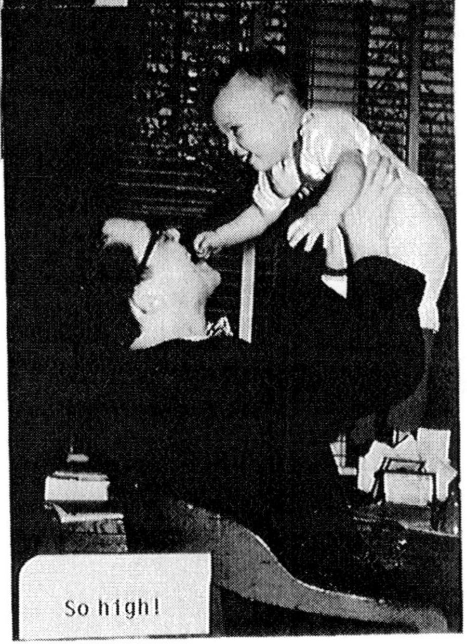

So high!

Our Family Christmas 1963

CHAPTER FOUR

ASSASSINATION OF PRESIDENT J. F. KENNEDY
AND
SUDDEN DEATH OF MY HUSBAND, WALT

Bonded with Christ Forever

"Blessed Are They that Mourn
for They Shall Be Comforted."

Matthew 5:4

The 50's had opened the door a tiny bit for women and other minorities when Barbara Walters became the first woman to write and help anchor the "Today Show" with the "old" greats like Dave Garraway and John Chancellor. Blacks were tired of not being allowed to sit at lunch counters or go into restaurants to eat. There were separate restrooms for blacks. "Coloreds" was the sign on the restroom doors. They were required to sit in the back of the bus, and to get up and let the whites sit down, until the day that Rosa Parks refused to give up her seat on the bus for a white person. This woman helped point the Civil Rights Movement in the right direction. In Montgomery, Alabama, bus boycotts began. Black schools were segregated and substandard. In the spring of *1954* the Brown *versus* Board of Education decision was passed (thanks to Justice Thurgood Marshall) making segregation illegal in schools.

It wasn't until *1957* that the first black students integrated our all white schools! Nine courageous black children integrated the Little Rock, Arkansas, High School. Out of fear and ignorance whites started building private schools for their kids, and the move to the suburbs began.

The 50's brought in the "duck tail" hair and leather jackets for young men; crew cuts were also in style. Elvis Presley and Little Richard revolutionized music for the young (and for some older) with Rock and Roll. They broke every rule of sound we considered "proper" for music, including the words, language and subject matter. It was shocking to see a person (Elvis the Pelvis, he was called) gyrating his hips in public, let alone on national television. Many considered it obscene. I remember how surprised and embarrassed I was watching gyrating hips on TV, and how loud and unpleasant the music was to my ears! What was happening to the world, we asked ourselves. Most thought surely the world was "going to hell in a hand basket."

In 1960 the world was ready to change. We voted in the first Roman Catholic and youngest President, John F. Kennedy. John Kennedy's election in 1960 had created a climate of compassion and idealism. He and Jackie were young and ambitious. There was not a more handsome, richer couple in all of the land. Most considered them the ultimate model of the perfect couple. Their reign at the White House was called "Camelot."

We were glued to the TV sets when Russian ships were steaming towards Cuba - a threat to our United States. Everyone was fearful of being blown up by Russia. After several days of threats by our new President, J. F. K., the ships reversed their course. I distinctly remember my fear when watching the ships and hearing the reports on television. This shook the whole country.

The threat of the atomic bomb, and the fear of communism were pervading our society. In certain areas of the country it was common to show anti-communism films. Bomb shelters were built and plans laid out in case of an atomic bomb attack.

People seemed to be coming around slowly to the plight of inequality. Maybe justice for all would come, we thought. This was why we had voted for Kennedy. Walt and I were becoming aware of others who did not have an equal chance as we did, and we did care. We were learning, and our sensitivity would sharpen as the years went by. We talked about a better society as the black students conducted lunch counter "sit-ins" and freedom demonstrations. These were non-violent and effective.

Desegregation was slowly beginning, led by the man who was to become the greatest man of peace and non-violence since Gandhi, Dr. Martin Luther King. In states like Mississippi and Alabama, blacks were registering to vote. But not without protests from white racists. There were white and black freedom fighters who put themselves on the line and died for the cause. The endurance of blacks was tested to the fullest, but they persisted. God was on their side and Dr. King was their faithful leader, encouraging them to endure even if they went to jail. Justice would be theirs, but *non-violence and persistence* was the only path to freedom. A better life with an equal chance was worth anything that could happen to them. It was 100 years after the Emancipation Proclamation and blacks did not have freedom yet. They had nothing to lose.

John Glenn went to the moon in 1962, yet we could not help so many who were poor, and who did not have a better way of life. Kennedy was becoming more assertive in the cause for equality, going out of his way, using his power as President of the United States to personally support Martin Luther King, having him released from jail, for example. Robert Kennedy, as Attorney General supported his brother in this crusade for justice.

In August of 1963 Washington D.C. saw an assembly of people the size and grandeur of which we had never seen before. Two hundred fifty thousand individuals came from all over the country, filling the Mall between the monuments, demonstrating their freedom to attain democracy for everyone. Members of many religious groups, black and white, Christian and Jew, came to participate and join hands in "Prayer Marches." Dr. King gave speeches pleading for equality. His words seldom leave my head - "I have a dream... Where little black boys and little black girls will be judged not by the color of their skin, but the content of their character." Carl Sandburg said "Nothing happens unless first a dream." Dr. King had a dream, and he passed that dream on to the world. There was hope for justice. We could all hold up our heads.

Then there came a violent wrenching of everyone's soul... I was shopping at the time. Suddenly the store erupted with loud noises and gasps. People were yelling, "the President's been shot!" "The President's been shot!" over and over again. I dashed out of the store and to my car. Home seemed far away, but somehow I got there. I couldn't believe what I was hearing. Maybe it was a hoax, I thought. As I quickly turned on the television, every channel had someone discussing the horrible scene of his assassination. Even newspeople were crying as they reported this tragedy! It was November 22, 1963, and in Dallas, Texas, John Fitzgerald Kennedy, our beloved President, was struck down by a single assassin's bullets.

It is so difficult to this day to absorb the idea that the one person, Lee Harvey Oswald, with his rifle could snuff out the life of this young leader who was trying hard to bring the nation to a peaceful co-existence. In his Inaugural Address Kennedy said: "Ask not what your country can do for you. Ask what you can do for your country." Those words left an impression on many people. The whole world sank into mourning... First it was shock and disbelief that this could have happened to such a promising leader.

He had come to the Presidency as a young, 46 year old leader with objectives that were not totally clear, but in three short years he was becoming a strong figure with well-defined goals. Some felt he prevented a third World War by his face to face discussion with Premier Khrushchev, as well as his "Ich Bin Ein Berliner" speech in Germany.

The fear of losing, morally and politically, left President Kennedy with a drive to bring peace and to put his beliefs into action.

He had a compassionate view of justice, as well as an unsympathetic view toward the Vietnam War. Our President was ready to bring home the troops who were dying by the thousands. He potentially could change our way of looking at what was most important. Peace and justice for all seemed close at hand. Most were equally excited by the prospects for this promising leader to end the fear of a nuclear holocaust. Walt and I had discussed these issues with other colleagues many times. It was on our minds constantly. We had hope for a just and peaceful world for our children. We had seen the birth of the "Peace Corps."

We had put "all our eggs in one basket" when we voted for this forceful leader. John F. Kennedy was our hope, and now our hopes were dashed to the winds. Many dreams died that day. In one terrible moment they were all gone... We grieved for the man who had become the pride of our nation and ourselves.

We cried for the dissension and lack of acceptance of others different from ourselves in the world. Our sorrow was deep for Jackie, Caroline and John for they would not have a husband and father anymore. How sad! We mourned for the millions for whom justice was delayed...

It seems that our tears would never stop, and even as I write this nearly thirty years later, my tears flow as they did for many days after his death. I have never mourned like that before. The whole seminary family mourned for the loss of our President. We shared a lot of feelings and were concerned for each other's welfare. Our only consolation was that God would get us through these difficult times.

The faculty was scheduled to have individual photos taken some days after Kennedy's assassination. It was noted, later, how one could see the grieving in their eyes. The spark in Walt's eyes had gone out. We read later that a Harris poll of the people's reaction after the assassination showed a profound change in what people were thinking. People in the government, led by President Lyndon B. Johnson, rejected extremism toward the right or the left. A sense of guilt for not being more accepting of people was the general reaction.

Our children were too young to understand what the country was experiencing. Tommy was going to be nine, Andy was seven, and

Gregory was going to be three. In those days we wanted to protect our children from unhappy things and felt it healthier for them emotionally if they did not know all the "bad" things that were happening in the world. The "problems" of the world were not generally openly discussed with the children. Most children never asked. Maybe it was because they knew we wanted them to be happy always. We would protect them with God's help. This was the way we had been raised, and were content with our attitudes and upbringing.

We were very involved with our sons' lives and education. Reading to them and they to us was a daily ritual when they were young. Family bicycle riding, roller and ice skating were favorites. These were things I did in my childhood days in North Dakota. Neither Walt nor I could swim well, but we insisted Andy and Tommy take swimming lessons when very young. We enjoyed playing softball and basketball as a family, usually going to the Seminary field house for basketball, until we put a hoop up in the backyard.

Walt immersed himself in writing. Concordia Publishing House had deadlines to follow and Walt needed to finish the manuscript on his first book of The Church in History series. The title was to be The Heirs of the Apostles. Marianka Fousek, a graduate student who worked under Walt, was editing for him.

Walt had not been feeling well for sometime. His headaches were becoming more frequent and more severe, but he rarely complained about them to me. Our friend, Dr. Mortensen, had put him in the hospital the year before and had done some tests because Walt had been having digestive problems. He was found to be without hydrochloric acid (which assists in digestion) in his stomach. Dr. Mortensen prescribed medication for the problem, and sent him home. The subject of headaches was discussed at that time, but the doctor concluded that since he was reading and studying so much it was natural to have a lot of headaches. That was the conclusion in 1963. Well, if that was the case, Walt figured he would just resign himself to having headaches.

In retrospect, I believe Walt *knew* there was something else wrong, but he wasn't saying anything. He used to kid me, telling me we would only have ten years of marriage. He would not live longer! This really upset me, needless to say. I believe he had a premonition about his death. I truly believe some people *know* when they are going to die. He also had several momentary bouts of blindness going back to Michigan days, and had seen an eye doctor at that time, but he did not give him any reason for concern. Walt again saw an ophthalmologist early in February of 1964. The doctor reported an increase in the pressure of the eyeball and some changes in the blood vessels in his eyes. There were other visual changes as well. This physician was deeply concerned and told Walt he needed to have more tests. Walt, however, was not quite ready to go again for more examinations. He wanted to get his manuscript finished, and was putting all his spare time into it.

Finally, he completed the manuscript on February 20. He was relieved and so was I! We did not go out and celebrate, but he and I participated in devotions (prayer and song) in one of the dorms at the seminary, as we did on occasion. (This prayer life brought students and faculty closer together.)

The next day, without a word of complaint or comment on how he was feeling, Walt walked the four blocks to the Seminary, lectured in his classes as usual, without anyone noticing any hesitation or pain (as the students told me later). He walked the four blocks home for lunch. I noticed he was tired and had pain, by just looking at his face. He only asked if I would lie down with him. I was concerned, but he appeared not to be. As an obedient wife, I did what he suggested. Tommy and Andy were in school and Gregory was taking his afternoon nap, so we had this quiet time together to lie down and rest. We discussed when he would go in for the tests the doctor requested. I knew he was in pain, but he always did things when *he* was ready and there was no changing that. This would be our last quiet time together.

It was about four o'clock and the boys would be coming home from school. When Walt got up from the bed he could barely stand - the pain in his head was so severe. I knew something had to be done *now*. There wasn't a 911 number to call in those days, so I called Doctor Mortensen's office. They said to bring him to the office. Looking back, it seems that he should have gone directly to an Emergency Room, even then, but unless you were critically ill, it was not usually done - certainly not the way emergency rooms are used today treating many minor situations. After calling my neighbor across the street, I helped Walt down the stairs. Each step was excruciating pain for him. It was at this time that God must have taken over. I do not know how we made it down those stairs. The agony for him, and the agony for me to have experienced this pain with him is difficult for me to express even now. God must have carried us both in His arms.

Somehow, in a haze I recall awakening Gregory from his nap. Tommy and Andy were just walking in the door from school, when Reverend and Mrs. Possehl came over from across the street. Decisions were made quickly. Mrs. Possehl took Tommy, Andy and Gregory to their home while Reverend Possehl helped me get Walt into the back seat of the car. We tried to lay him down, but the pain was too severe. He was not saying anything, but kept moving his head as if to rid himself of the pain. The doctor's office was only 20 minutes away, but it seemed forever. Walt even walked into the doctor's office with just our help. Where all three of us got the strength could only have come from God.

Walt was immediately put in one of the examining rooms to lie down. I recall Dr. Mortensen ordering a shot for pain. Walt was lying there without saying anything. The pain continued as before, making him very restless. I vividly remember sitting there at the head of the examining table feeling totally helpless and alone, unable to do anything to ease his pain. Everyone was busy, it seemed. With the shot given, they assumed it was a matter of time before the pain would subside. The doctor was sure it was a *migraine headache*, and we were told not to worry. They left us alone, but nurses looked in frequently to see how he was. It seemed like an eternity. The shot only made him groggy but the pain persisted. Dr. Mortensen at last finished seeing the rest of his patients and came in to see Walt. He was concerned that the pain had not subsided, and decided that Walt needed to go to the hospital for tests. He still comforted us with the thought that it was probably a migraine.

I rode in the ambulance with Walt to Lutheran Hospital on Miami and Potomac Streets. We were going back to the hospital where I had graduated from nursing 10 years earlier. Now it seemed long ago.

They put him on the nursing division where our friend from North Dakota, Lori Duesenberg, was Head Nurse. She had graduated several years earlier and had worked her way up to achieve this position. She and Bob had been married six months earlier and Lori was pregnant with her first child. Lori was to care for her Bob's best friend and my husband, a task she accepted with confidence, knowing too, that the Lord was present to guide her.

Walt was settled into a private room. Lori was not on duty when we arrived, but I called her immediately and talked with both her and Bob. Walt was resting a bit better and it was getting late. No tests would be done anymore that evening because of the late hour. (That was the way it was years ago.) It was Friday night, and the weekend was upon us.

Several of Walt's colleagues came late that evening after hearing about my concern. We were all worried. The last word from the doctor was that Walt had a severe *migraine headache*, but more diagnostic tests would be done.

When that terrible day was over, I gathered my boys from the Possehls' and, exhausted, we went to bed. I assured them that Daddy would be okay, and he would be home from the hospital soon. We prayed hard for him, with the hope that God and the doctors would make him well.

The next day was Saturday and friends called to take the boys into their homes. Andy and Tommy stayed with our neighbors again and Gregory stayed at Don and Corinne Deffners' for several days, as I recall. How thankful I was for those kind friends who, with their deep love and concern, helped me along the way.

That morning when I called the hospital and was told they were running some tests, they did not sound concerned. Walt had a fair night, they said. I shopped for groceries and got to the hospital around 10 a.m. Walt was not looking good. The color in his face, and the painful look in his eyes told me this was a critical situation. He was extremely restless and could not speak coherently. The pain killers had reached his brain, but not his pain. He was worse than when I had left him the night before, I thought. I fought back the tears. I did not want Walt to see my worry and fears. After futile attempts were made to do an EEG (Electroencephalogram), fear overwhelmed me. To see his pain was unbearable. I left the room in tears. What was happening to him? No doctor was around, but Lori was there. Here was our friend who could give me some answers. She told me that Dr. Mortensen had done a spinal tap earlier; the spinal fluid was bloody and the pressure was high. There was a problem somewhere in the head, possibly a tumor. These were the most terrifying words I could hear - brain tumor. I had seen the "vegetable garden" at Barnes Hospital a few years earlier as a student nurse. This was the place where many people waited to die after failed brain surgery. "Wasn't there a woman in her 30's still at Lutheran

Hospital where a dozen years earlier she had been admitted with a brain tumor?" I inquired of Lori. Yes. She was still lying there "vegetating," while her husband visited every day, praying for her to die. I was devastated. There was not a thing I could do to help. My years of nursing could not help take away this deadly tumor.

I stayed out of Walt's room until I quit crying. I *must* be strong, I told myself. He must not know how upset I am. What would he think? There he is in all this pain, and I am doing the crying! I could only hold his hand and pray quietly. He could not communicate anymore. "Wasn't it just *yesterday* when we had our last conversation?", I thought to myself. That seemed like a long time ago. Walt had waited *too long*, and I was *too patient* with his delaying. He could not tell me he was sorry, nor I him. Now it was too late.

Our dear friend Bob Duesenberg came to be with us. He was always a tower of strength, and to this day has never changed. He never gave way to tears, but he and Lori were there for me, as they have always been. We were there for each other - bonded together. With our courage and faith in God, we would get through this terrifying time.

Bob and I sat in disbelief at Walt's discomfort, totally helpless, too shocked to pray. Lori was with other patients. Suddenly Walt quit breathing. In desperation to revive him, Bob jumped up on the bed and began artificial respiration, while in horror I watched, frantically calling out for Lori's help. An emergency team intubated him, and the machine began breathing for him. It seemed for a while that they had resuscitated him, but he was not breathing on his own. He had really died. He seemed at peace at last. Somehow this was a relief for all of us because he was *no longer suffering*. "Thanks be to God!" was all I could utter at the time.

After that the world around me seemed to stop. I recall only glimpses of people passing through my mind, a flash of friends stopping by; Dr. Fuerbringer, President of the Seminary, friends and colleagues visiting. I was in a world of haze, medicated to ease the agony. There were several nurse friends I recall who stayed day and night for the next few days: Elsa Meyer, Elsie Lange, and Miriam Timm Greene. Lori and Bob seemed always to be there with me. It is just now as I am putting this in writing, that I am realizing all the wonderful support I received from so many people during that terrible time. Some have never talked about those few days until just recently. It may be too painful, while others may still feel the loss. There are just some things too difficult to talk about, but they cannot be forgotten. I hope writing about it will help me put it away, once and for all.

I gathered my sons together after that tragic day and brought them home. How does one tell little boys they will no longer have a Daddy? That he would not come home from the hospital? That their Daddy was dying, and was soon going to live in heaven with Jesus? Even though we wanted him here, he was with God, God would take care of him, and Daddy would be singing with all those wonderful angels. We prayed for Daddy, but God was ready for him in heaven. We each must wait for that grand reunion with Him. While we are here on earth, I said I would take good care of them, with the help of God. We would be fine. I would try hard to be their Daddy and Mommy now. We would love each other and stay together. I held Gregory close as the tears were streaming down my face. Tommy and Andy sitting close by me, did not cry as I talked, but were quiet and sad. Were they too young to really comprehend? Or maybe they did, but weren't able to express their feelings. It had to be unreal for them too. Had they not lost a number of father figures in the past? This one too was just passing through, and now he had also left them. How could I possibly repair the pain of their losses? Mine was so great. I mourn for them yet today.

Gregory had just turned three February 4th. He certainly would miss his Daddy. This precious little one Walt and I had wanted with all our heart would feel this loss in the years to come. He was so special and God had truly blessed us. Gregory only knew that his Daddy was gone, but he could not comprehend why. He would ask for him many times in the days that followed. After awhile he quit asking because it would always make Mommy cry. What does that do to a child? He would always come and give me lots of hugs and tell me not to cry. He wanted Mommy to be happy again. There is no way I can express the sadness I felt. My sons would no longer have their Daddy - and I wondered how I could ever take his place.

Our parents and families were called after that first night. Friends, colleagues, and students communicated with other friends all over the country. Our families were spread out far and wide as they had always been (and still are today). My Mom and Dad came those 100 miles from Jacksonville, Illinois, to be with us. Mama stayed close and slept with me that first lonely, sad night. Dad even slept on the sofa to take the phone calls and answer the door when families would arrive.

This was the second shock for all of us in just three months. With Kennedy's death, he also left a young family with a three-year-old son. Walt would have been 35 in two months. This was another loss of a young professor from Concordia Seminary. Mourning had become a way of life for those dear friends.

It was early Monday morning, February 24, 1964, when they pulled the plug on the resuscitator. Walt was gone at 34 years of age, now only a memory... I was a 32-year-old widow. Mom and Dad Oetting had arrived the night before. We were together in their bedroom when the phone call came from the hospital. There were no questions asked. The medical team had used their best judgment. There are no words to express the grief we all felt at that moment. Dad Oetting, who never believed in crying, shed his first tears in our presence. I was grief stricken for Mother Oetting as well. No one can fully comprehend a mother's grief at the loss of her child. She had loved and nurtured all of her children. Walt was her first born, and *so* special to her and to Dad Oetting as well. Walt had been born on April 25, 1929 on his Dad's birthday. He had made them both so proud. Their grief cannot be expressed within the pages of a book. It was only sealed in the soul until death relieved the pain.

My parents' grief was for me and for my boys too. They were not as close emotionally to Walt, as we had lived miles apart all our married life. They were there for me, always sharing my sorrow and lifting the burden. Mom and Dad came to be my constant helpers and support during those years as a widow. They were always available for whatever need I had with my sons. I owe them so much. At this writing my father is also gone (he died in 1985), and my mother, who is 86 years old, is finding life a constant struggle. There is still sadness and grief in her heart for the many losses in her family. She, too, forgets how much of herself she has given to her family all these years. She is precious to me.

The Seminary family simply showered me with their love. How else can one express the gratitude I feel yet today. I guess food must be an important part of grieving. It came from everywhere! At least we all were relieved of cooking for awhile. I had no appetite and had to be urged to eat. To this day, I vividly remember Joanne Michael Lanser in her own kind, assertive way pushing food and drink on me when we were preparing to attend Walt's funeral. I am thankful for dear friends like her. She told me later that she sat with me for hours. Fatigue and grief just left me totally at a loss for anything this earth had to give me. This pain and emptiness gave me a feeling of constant nausea. I needed to cry a lot more, but there was not enough time. So many people came to talk and to express their feelings of loss as well. I felt I needed to be on top of things if at all possible, and I wanted to be able to talk about Walt and his death. I could recite the events of the past days, but it was difficult to put the feeling behind it. It was like telling a story, like a dream that happened. The doctor gave me tranquilizers to carry me through those days. I was grateful for that because then I could sleep. It numbed some of my feelings, but I don't believe I could have made it through without the medication. I felt I could get through the days anyway. God was carrying me and giving me the strength from moment to moment. I am so thankful for my faith and for my dependence upon Him. I am a living example of how *God does* get you through the most trying times. He knows your grief and *He* is your constant help. "Surely He has borne our griefs and carried our sorrows..." Isaiah 53:4. I did not have to ask our Heavenly Father, for He was always there just holding me up. I still have that same faith and closeness to Him today.

Members of the Seminary faculty, under Dean Repp's guidance came to the house and with the advice of our fathers and Walt's brother, Louis, a memorial service and a funeral were planned for two days later. He was to be buried at Our Redeemer Cemetery in St. Louis County close to where Dr. Walter A. Maier, world-renowned Lutheran Hour speaker, who had also taught at Concordia Seminary, was buried, along with his wife, Hulda. Bob and Dick Duesenberg's father had been laid to rest in that same cemetery 25 years earlier. Many of the old professors and Synodical presidents were buried at Concordia Cemetery, an older cemetery in the city, along with Mother Oetting's family, the Nolkempers and many of her relatives. I was informed that there were problems with vandalism, and Our Redeemer Cemetery would be more suitable.

Since 1964, Our Redeemer Cemetery laid to rest Mom and Dad Oetting, Mom and Dad Brauer, and numerous Brauer relatives, as well as Professor and Dorothy Bartling, the Hoyers, the Klincks, and some of the other professors and wives who have passed on. A large gathering of saints on earth lie there together in wait for the Resurrection.

When I think back on those days, I can't believe I could even pick out a casket. A steel grey one was selected and the price was right. By this time, Bob Duesenberg, our dear lawyer friend, had taken over all my financial matters. I had no idea about *anything*. Was there life insurance, pension? Walt had taken care of all these matters. After all, he wasn't *planning* to die, so he had not told me anything about our finances and investments. Fortunately, he kept good records and Bob was able to go through all the papers of this man's life time. I am forever grateful and thank God every day for a friend like Bob.

He and Lori would come over and he would go through papers, while Lori and I talked and cried together. These were very special times, bonding us together in a friendship that is sealed forever. Since those days we always seek each other out, and have cried on each other's shoulders hundreds of times. Truer friends were never had by anyone. We always know we have each other.

Walt's body was lying in state for two days and nights at the Beiderweiden Funeral Home. This was the funeral home that many good Lutherans chose to care for their dead. The owners were also Lutheran.

They had reserved a huge room for all the mourners to come and "pay their respects" to my husband. I remember little about those days and evenings except that many people came from around the country. Family, friends, relatives, colleagues, students, classmates, members from our congregation in Michigan came standing in line to stare in disbelief, to wonder, and to give my family and me their love and sympathy. I was in another world and God was holding me up. I never seemed to tire as long as I was with people. I was neither hungry nor thirsty. Every bit of energy was spent in talking with so many whom I love, and for their just being with us, I am eternally grateful to them all.

Tommy, Andy and Gregory were there short periods of time. They were on their best behavior, but they did not understand the meaning of it all. Gregory says now that he recalls nothing about his father or anything of those sad days. Tommy and Andy remain silent, though their loss too must have been incomprehensible.

The following Wednesday afternoon Concordia Seminary had a Memorial Service for Walt in their Chapel. The whole room was overflowing with colleagues who loved him. Many students came to give their last tribute to a professor whom they admired. Not until later in reading their written cards and letters did I realize how close they felt to him. Walt had several large seminar classes with 100 students attending. Every now and then one still will be in touch with me just to let me know what they felt about their professor.

Months later a student, John Truebenbach, whose avocation was photography, presented me with an envelope of numerous 8 x 10 photos he had taken the previous November - pictures of Walt in the classroom teaching and pictures of Walt and Greg at home. A total surprise! I had no knowledge of these pictures being taken. How precious, how moving! They were in albums until a few years ago when Greg asked me to have them framed for his home. Now Greg and his father hang on our walls, cherished memories of a special time. I do not believe I have ever gotten over the loss of our President and my husband - two men I considered great men of potential who could have changed many things, including my whole way of life...

The following is the most beautiful and comforting sermon I have ever heard. It was given by Professor Gilbert Thiele, Head of the Historical Theology Department, for the memorial service. I feel a need to share it with you readers, for many of you have had loved ones who are gone. I have referred back to this sermon these many years as loved ones have passed, to remind me again and again that we are bonded with Christ forever. May you always be comforted as well.

O God the Father in heaven, have mercy upon us;

O God the Son, Jesus Christ, Redeemer of the world, have mercy upon us;

O God the Holy Ghost, the Comforter, have mercy upon us and grant us Thy peace.

Amen.

Isaiah 40:11. *He shall feed His flock like a shepherd; He shall gather the lambs with His arm and carry them in His bosom; and shall gently lead those that are with young.*

St. John 10:11, *I am the Good Shepherd; the Good Shepherd giveth His life for the sheep.*

27-30. *My sheep hear My voice and I know them and they follow Me; and I give unto them eternal life and they shall never perish; neither shall any pluck them out of My hand. My Father which gave them Me is greater than all, and none is able to pluck them out of My Father's hand. I and the Father are One.*

Reverend and dear fathers, brothers, sons, and daughters, dear family and friends in Christ.

I have seen him living.

I have seen him working.

I have seen him growing as a man, as a Christian, as a teacher.

And now, I have seen him dying, and I have seen him die.

Walter was born the same year that I entered the seminary. Both of us, for certain periods of time during our ministry, served in parishes. His path and mine first crossed at a conference in Michigan in 1957. Thus the process of the intertwining of our careers and lives in our church, and then since 1959 at this school, began. I think, then, that I speak for everyone here: I need hope and comfort, as do my colleagues and you the family, as much as anyone.

So I would have you with me seek to draw strength, hope, and comfort from these words, taken as they are out of both covenants of the Sacred Scriptures, from the Old Testament, from the man we call the Evangelist of the Old Covenant, and from the New Testament, from St. John. These words, Isaiah 40:11, St. John 10:11, 27-30, today speak to us of

SHEPHERD AND SHEEP - THE SAVING BOND OF LIFE THAT NEVER DIES

First it must be said that when we speak of our Blessed Lord, the Saviour, as Shepherd, we are dealing with a remarkable paradox and a shift in roles. Just this morning in this chapel a sermon was preached on a passage from the first chapter of St. John, the words of John the Baptist, pointing to our Lord, and saying, "Behold, the Lamb of God." Yet - our Lord gave Himself the title "Shepherd" and unquestionably gave to His followers the name "sheep and lambs." There must be some deep reason for this, that He can take upon Himself the role of one who unites Himself to His flock as shepherd really only after He has completely fulfilled His *first* assignment as the Lamb, obedient, tractable, ready to be offered. Then He could become the shepherd, and establish with His sheep a bond of life that neither breaks nor dies. We belong to Him in his role of shepherd which succeeds His labor, victorious as it is, as the Lamb, by the right of the redemption that He has achieved.

Everyone likes to have a claim on somebody else, and when we have established a firm claim, especially on someone whom we love, we do not want to see it ever end. When a claim has been established upon us by someone good, and strong, we would like it to last forever. The bond between the shepherd and His sheep, established as it is by the redemption that He has achieved, is such a bond that *never* ends. There are all kinds of similes, metaphors, figures of speech used in the Bible about this, that God sends His Son to be the Redeemer of the world. But all of them have, in one way or another, the idea of purchase, gift, offering, sacrifice, rescue, embedded deeply in them. The very words "redeem", "reclaim", and whatever other synonyms you may know of, all have this in them. When you can speak of yourselves, as the family, of yourselves as colleagues, of yourselves as students and friends, or when we can speak of *him*, as members of the flock of God, this is only and always because of what the Saviour Himself has first done.

This is outlined in John 10:11, "I am the Good Shepherd; the Good Shepherd giveth His life for the sheep." This applies to all of us surely, but let us think now primarily of Walter. He *was* His, and *is* His, because of an incalculable price, an unspeakable labor, and an everlasting effort on the part of the Shepherd to add *him* to the number of His own dear sheep. This claim and the right of possession of the Shepherd over us all, His sheep, and above all now over Walter, is not merely something that happened and then just blandly continues. No, it is more.

The verse from Isaiah makes this clear: *When sheep belong to the Shepherd, and the Shepherd has established His claim upon them by the right of His redemption, then He continuously works in their behalf.* Four wonderful words are used: *feed, gather, carry, lead.* No doubt they each have their individual application. Certainly it should not be foregone to mention that in each individual's life the application of the redemption, and the establishment of the lasting claim of the shepherd upon His sheep, begins with the washing of the water in the Word. Of this we are convinced. But again, it does not stop there. I think, perhaps most of all now, of Walter's three boys and their mother, and with them, especially of these words: *"He shall gather the lambs with His arm and carry them in His bosom, and shall gently lead those that are with young."* Where would you, dear sister and daughter in Christ, with those boys, be able to find any sense, any meaning, any direction for tomorrow, and tomorrow, and tomorrow, except in just such an assurance that He will work *for* you, *with* you in your behalf. You can be certain that the boys will not be desolate orphans. While they have lost their father, they will nevertheless be in the very closest association with a Shepherd who has established with them, as He did with him, their father, and has with you, a bond so deep, so thorough, that we can call it literally everlasting. *For the bond between the Lord, the Shepherd, and Walter, His sheep, whom we mourn, is not severed.* Why then should it be severed between Him and you? Between Him and the boys? For that matter, between the Shepherd and us all? I suppose that occasions of this kind do not happen very often, where there can be a participation, a sharing in your immediate need and grief by so many. Thus all of us, his parents, your parents, the boys, our students, our clergy, our faculty, can find strength. Where will we find nourishment when we feel as starved as we do now? Where will we find a haven unless it is He who gathers us with His arm? Where will we find security unless, like sheep and lambs, we are gathered into that big bulky fold in the garment of the shepherd of the East as He picks us up? And where will we find any goal left after the shock which we have had in the last five days if He does not lead us as though we were still young or still expecting children? This evidence of the continuous effort on the part of an ever-present Christ for us who remain indicates that *the bond never breaks or dies.*

In John, to go back again to the 27th to the 30th verses, we find assurance that death itself is not strong enough to break the bond, our Lord says: "My sheep hear my voice, I know them, and they follow Me, and I give unto them eternal life, and they shall never perish, neither shall any pluck them out of My hand." We all feel somehow or another that we have become the victims of a monstrous deprivation, for we have lost someone whom we have loved, and who we know loved us. *It is good to remember that in the memory of those who remain the bond*, also in a very real sense, *remains unbroken*. The not distinctively Christian immortality, of being remembered by those whom we have left behind, which serves a purpose and has its place -- nevertheless a serviceable and good one -- is surpassed by the fact that the universal depriver, death, that takes away from us the normal everyday God-given joys of existence, cannot sever the bond between those who die and Him who saved them. *Our whole faith*, the entire bulk, and depth, and structure of our most holy religion, *is ultimately dependent on this truth that the severance, the deprivation, the incision into life that death really is, for him who dies and for his Saviour is a reunion, not a separation.*

This, it appears to me, is of *unspeakably great comfort for all of us*. Always, but especially in cases of sudden death, the very word that Jesus uses is applicable - that somebody is plucking these people right out of our lives. We would like to hang onto them, and our hands are empty. Not so the divine hands of the Saviour -- they are not empty. No death, no evil, no Satan, no hell *can* pluck Walter, *has* plucked him, or can pluck any of us out of the masterful yet tender hands of the shepherd. This is the way we must *think* about this death too, that Walter has in a very real sense been commended, as so many passages in the Scripture attest, into the hands of God. "Father, into Thy hands," our Lord said. Stephen said something similar. For generations of Christians as they have time and the occasion all through their lives and then on their deathbed to say it, this is what helps them: *that they are always in the hands of Christ who will never relinquish them.*

But there is something even greater, if that be possible, than knowing that *the bond between the shepherd and His sheep, between Jesus and Walter, between Jesus Christ* and *all of ourselves, is a saving bond of life that never breaks or dies*. This is in full harmony with the ultimate force and power of the revelation of God in His son, Jesus Christ: that is *that all things must glorify the Father*. Our Lord Himself puts it this way: "My Father which gave them Me is greater than all, and none is able to pluck them out of My Father's hand. I and My Father are one." We can say then such words as abound in the hymnody of the church, for instance, "Asleep in Jesus" or any other words of hope with every measure of confidence in the fact that this shepherd is a living, regnant, welcoming Saviour. While He is in our midst He is also at the right hand of God, receiving unto Himself those who were His on earth. It is true that the one who lived, who died, who rose, who ascended is the one that lived for *us*, who died for *us* and ascended that *we* might follow Him into His mansions. The opposite is unthinkable because this is all true, then *we also belong to the Father* who sent *Him*. This is probably as close as we can get in a situation of this kind to any reasonable satisfaction for our minds and for the future. Please -- let us not try to discover the ultimate reason behind an event of this kind -- it will elude us. We will despair in the search for an ultimate solution. But we know, and this is as rock-ribbed and as certain not only as anything as we will discover, but as certain as anything that has been revealed by God to us, *this is God's way with His children*. We here in the Seminary have gone through this kind of experience all too often by human standards; five young men in the last ten years in their late twenties or early thirties have been snatched, the way we put it, out of our midst, and every time it is just as hard and maybe harder to square away over against this kind of a thing. Perhaps one way of looking at it is this: very few men are allowed by God to finish their work so soon. If this be true, that *what God wanted him to do is finished*, (*there is no need now of rehearsing the catalog of his activities, or of his achievements*) then we can take comfort in this, that he is, as it were, taken by the Saviour's hands and turned over to the Father's. When you are with Christ, you are with God. It is the same.

The saving bond of life that never breaks or dies. A life bestowed upon us through baptism, nourished by Word and Sacrament, somehow or another supported and fostered also through our own prayers and devotions and work under God's blessing -- things for him have changed less than they have improved. For us it might be very difficult for a while. But knowing this, that the same Saviour into whose hand *he* has now been commended is also *our* abiding shepherd and never-failing companion and living Lord, we can say:

I have seen him living,
I have seen him working,
I have seen him studying,
I have seen him teaching,
I have seen him growing as a man and as a teacher, and as a Christian.

Each one of us can say this. But then we should conclude: Now let us in God's name get on with the business of living and working until this same shepherd calls us unto Himself.

O God, the Father in heaven, have mercy upon us;
O God, the Son, Jesus Christ, Redeemer of the world,
have mercy upon us;
O God, the Holy Ghost, the Comforter, have mercy upon us
and grant us Thy peace. +

Amen

Soli Deo Gloria

* * * * * * * * * * *

Thursday, February 27, was the large funeral for Walt at Resurrection Lutheran Church. This is the church where we held our membership and this was where he assisted Pastor George Sommermeyer in preaching and teaching Bible Class. Walt had classes of over 100 parishioners eager to learn about the Bible and its history each Sunday. Pastor Sommermeyer assisted by our friend Reverend Herb Hohenstein provided a beautiful service and sermon. The Schola Cantorum Choir of Concordia Seminary, under the direction of Walt's classmate and colleague, Professor Robert Bergt, with student James

Brauer at the organ, sang and played the most comforting hymns. Music is truly the most comforting and uplifting to the saddest of hearts.

It was appropriate to have final tributes to Walt's existence in this beautiful place. This church had just been built and dedicated to the Lord a year or so before. Pastor Sommermeyer, his wife Gertrude, and members were so kind and showered us with their support and love. After the burial they provided a wonderful meal for all our families and friends. Their kindnesses are remembered these many years. Walt was laid to rest that day in that tranquil place, Our Redeemer Cemetery on Mackenzie Road.

His battle on this earth was done. This saint who from his labors was at rest...

Requiescat In Pace.

FOOTPRINTS

One night a man had a dream, and in his dream he reviewed the footsteps he had taken in his life.

He looked and noticed that all over the mountains and difficult places that he had traveled there was one set of footprints;

but over the plains and down the hills, there were two sets of footprints, as if someone had walked by his side.

He turned to Christ and said, "There is something I don't understand.

Why is it that down the hills and over the smooth and easy places you have walked by my side;

but, here over the tough and difficult places I have walked alone, for I see in those areas there is just one set of footprints."

Christ turned to the man and said, "It is that while your life was easy I walked along your side;

but here, where the walking was hard and the paths were difficult, was the time you needed Me most, and that is why I carried you."

CHAPTER FIVE

WIDOWHOOD - WORLD CHANGING AND RAISING THREE SONS - MEETING DON MOVING TOWARD EQUALITY

"He shall gather the lambs
with His arm
And carry them in His bosom,
And shall gently lead those
that are with young."

Isaiah 40:11

Looking back on those days and feeling those moments when time stopped have been the best therapy I could ever give to myself, and a gift to my family. Now it is written for history, never to be forgotten. *Now* I can put it aside, and go on with my life.

In one short week this person who was the driving force in my life seemed to be completely eradicated. Walt was an unwritten memory. It was not very fair to him or to the family just to let go like that, I felt. I recall being stunned when I looked in his closet and in his drawers after the families had gone. There was nothing left! The families felt it of utmost importance for us emotionally not to hold on to his things, but that we must get on with our lives and try to forget him. I agreed in theory. A few special things like some ties, cuff links, some books, and his Masters Hood, were saved for my sons in one large box, and some of these would be given to them on special days like Confirmation and Graduation.

Within a short period of time Dean Repp wanted me to go through Walt's office, clean out his desk, and select books I wanted to save. They would need to clear the office for another professor who would be taking his place.

I spent hours trying to figure out who would like special books from Walt. The librarian, James Michael, at the Seminary and "Father Phil," Walt's colleague and friend in the next office were asked to assist in this enormous task. Numerous books I autographed in Walt's memory. I tied together many books to give later to family, colleagues, students and friends. He had well over 1,000 volumes, including a complete collection of Russian works, as Walt's Washington University friend and mentor Dr. Weltin informed me. The remaining books were taken to Concordia Seminary library, some sold, and many given away. Little money was received by me.

We received cards, letters, and telegrams from so many people around the country. These I put into a large scrapbook immediately. It was a comfort to do this. The memorials went for many charities including the Seminary. Some were designated for my boys' education but that amount was small; they were yet so young. There were a lot of flowers sent which were beautiful, but they passed all too soon.

Dr. Repp, Dean of the Seminary, stopped by one day while I was going through memorials. He was letting me know I should be thinking about where I was going to live, and if at all possible, could we move by April. He informed me that they wanted again to paint and clean the house for the new professor who was coming. I don't need to tell anyone that I had *not even thought* of moving yet! He did not offer any suggestions at that point either. It just had not occurred to me that I should be thinking of moving so soon. Yes, I assured him, I understood, now that he informed me. It was certainly in order that I would move eventually. Reality struck me down to earth that day!

Now that our husband and father was gone, certainly we were not needed. Instantly I felt *very unimportant* and insignificant. That singular thought stuck in my mind for many years to come. True, my children certainly needed and loved me the most, and I them. They were my motivation for existence, but it did not change the fact that once my husband was gone, I was not an important consideration.

I noticed then and still do notice the status of many single women, widowed or divorced. This personal experience has sensitized me to their treatment by society. There *was* and *still is* a lack of awareness of the needs of others who are different. Wouldn't it be great to be able to step into another person's shoes, if even for a moment and to feel what they feel? *Then* for them to express the hurt and how it made *them* feel at *that* moment. We diligently pray for the widows and orphans in our churches, but after that we in society do not know what to with them. It isn't that society doesn't care, but people are eager to get on with life - enough of all this psychologizing!

Well, after several formal calls by Dean Repp over a month's time, I figured I should dry the tears, and start looking for a place for the four of us to live. I knew I was getting angry about all these events that were certainly not my fault! I was especially upset about the Dean pressuring me to come up with another place to live so soon. It would have been nice if some tangible suggestions, and some emotional support were offered. It would have been good therapy for all of us.

We were certainly hurting and in need. In those days, some considered therapy as a sign of weakness, and a lack of faith in God. I certainly did not want to be thought of as anything but a tower of strength and a woman of courage! Down deep I was frustrated and feeling inadequate for the overwhelming task of being mother and father to three growing sons. After all, this was not in synchronization with the whole plan in life that society expected of me. I had found a good husband, married, had children, and was a good wife and mother. I felt I had done everything right. So now what was expected of me was just a bit much, I thought.

Well, I tried to put my angry and sad feelings on the back burner (so to speak), and began looking in the paper for places to rent. Walt had life insurance and a pension plan. With the Social Security we received, we had enough with which to live, plus some to invest. Interest rates were 4% on secure investments. Bob Duesenberg who was advising me in everything (I respected his advice totally), said that was the way to go. (It's amazing that nearly thirty years later we are again back to such low interest rates.)

We got along fine on the income. Our life style was never "fancy" or expensive. My boys would need money for college, so it was important to be frugal as Walt had been, I told myself. I had been cutting my sons' hair for years - the old "butch" haircut, until I learned how to style their hair in the longer look with a comb and scissors. I did Don's hair later too. We always "made do" like our parents had done before. Bob had handled all the finances. I knew how to write a check and that was it. Bob was a good teacher, and if I would get over my feelings of inadequacy for this task before me, I could do it, I told myself. They say if you can get mad enough you can do anything. By nature, I had always been a happy, rather humorous, optimistic person with a sensitive and sentimental soul. So revving up anger was not natural for me, and to say why I was angry was even harder. Today, it comes easily, and I never mind telling people how I feel. Aging and maturity have done wonders for me.

God did answer my prayers. No matter what happened in life, my faith in Him would be there. I knew He was carrying us. Look what we had been through in a short time! We were alive and well, and now we just had to have a plan... A new way of life. It was not easy to figure out.

Our good neighbors told us about the recent death of an elderly widow on Clayton Road. Her house was located across our alley and would eventually be available. But the estate had to be settled first. Praise the Lord for good neighbors! Mr. Wotka was the owner of this nice home, which was right across from the Cheshire Inn on Clayton Road. He said he would get the estate settled quickly, so we could move in soon.

What a perfect location! And this kind man was only asking $150.00 a month rent for this house with three bedrooms. It was a comfortable two story home with a garage in back. How nice! My boys could still have the same playmates, and the distance to Bethel Lutheran School would be the same. How thankful we were. God *was truly* helping the four of us at every turn.

Packing was started immediately. His house would be available the end of April, and there was a lot to do. The Seminary kindly put the word out that help would be needed to move us. Some furniture would have to be sold or given away. We were going into a smaller place, and did not need the office furniture. Walt had a solid oak desk and chair which I gave away or sold to one of my preacher brothers-in-law. (Now I wish I had them back to give to Gregory.) An entire wall of books and bookshelves were given away. I saved and boxed some books for us to keep, many of which were cherished art and literature books.

Walt's colleagues, their wives, students and friends were so helpful in cleaning the house which was to be our new home (as we had all done for Professor Reimann's widow, Margaret, the year before). A very large job was removing the wall-to-wall carpeting (which we had purchased from the previous owner) from this big house, having it cut, cleaned and placed in the new house, after removing thousands of tacks! I vividly recall Walt's colleague, Robert Conrad, fitting and laying the stairs carpeting in our future home - a very big job! The Seminary did not wish to buy it from me, and since I did not have the money to buy new carpeting, it was worth the effort to have this cherished covering for our floors.

The big moving day was set for a weekend at the end of April, so everyone would be free. What a wonderful bunch of people came to move us that day in April. Our little family of four moved to our new home at 6963 Clayton Road just "across the alley from the Alamo," if you will. As we settled into our new home on Clayton Road, the life which was unfolding before me took on a deeper meaning. We were beginning to realize what our day to day existence would be like without a husband and father. However sad it was for us, we had at least made a giant step moving out of one way of life and into another.

Those three years in the lovely home on Alamo had gone all too quickly. We had God, family and lots of friends who had sustained us during those months and years. "For to him that is joined to all the living there is hope," it says in Ecclesiastes 9:4. How true! I was a good wife to

Walt for nine and one-half years. I had lived *before* I knew him, so there was hope for life *after* him.

What I had not anticipated was the pent-up gradual release of angry feelings by Tommy and Andy. To be again without a father cast another blanket of insecurity over them. It began with slipping in school. They seemed less interested in their responsibilities, as well as at home and toward family. They expressed it through increasingly open expressions of anger and rebellious behavior as they became older. Andy and Tommy were at the impressionable ages of eight and nine years, and without a father to model after. They had a father for only five years, and then he too was gone.

Gregory, too, at three years of age knew he did not have a daddy. He sometimes would cry a little when I was crying, but he would always give me a big hug and assume the role as my comforter. As he grew, his feelings of loss too would grow and take on a deeper meaning for him. He began spending a lot of time looking through photo albums. He would study the pictures, and try to feel who his father was, but he said little to me about it. He did not ask many questions, but wanted to figure it out in his young mind. He did this later through looking at our slides, spending hours just searching to know this important person in his life whom he had missed.

As he grew into the teen years, when he had spare moments, he continued to do this searching, trying to identify as much as possible with his father. Did this man in these pictures really love him like Mother and family would tell him? So many friends have told him now how much he has taken on his father's appearance. It amazes me so much that even Walt's mannerisms seem to be innate in Greg. It saddens me deeply to write about my little Gregory's "search" for his unknown Daddy. He had such a need to know. Did he really find out enough for himself? He has never said. My heart still cries for him and for Tommy and Andy. I feel they were cheated out of a terrific father. Tommy and Andy were older when he died and remembered what their Daddy was like. They kept busy with school and friends and appeared to carry on fairly well in their daily living.

"For in Thee the fatherless find mercy." Hosea 14:3. This was their hope and my confidence, and truly, "Blessed are they that mourn for they shall be comforted." Matthew 5:4. I received comfort from Helmut

Thielickes' book Out of the Depths, which I had read just weeks before Walt's death. How God does guide us into His path...

Time had passed and the reality of what *really* did happen to Walt was hitting me. I *needed* to know more about this brain tumor that had taken away this thirty-four year old man of mine. He was so young and seemingly healthy. He had not lost weight or looked sickly. He had been mentally alert and had not missed a thought or sentence, according to what his students and colleagues would tell me later.

I needed to talk with his doctor and our friend, Dr. Mortensen. He and Diana invited me to their home one evening. I was pleased that he understood how important it was for me to know everything about that tumor, before I could totally accept this terrible loss. They were gracious in sitting with me for a number of hours while I asked questions. He explained that this non-malignant tumor was in the third ventricle of the brain, which he said was not an operable area. It would have been too damaging and dangerous to try. Possibly it would have left him in a vegetative state, that dreaded suspension between life and death. The tumor was small, and it was suspended on a chain. Like a ball and chain, this tumor swung into the respiratory foramen (or hole). In one single moment, that tumor, large enough to obliterate the opening, immediately "knocked out" his respiratory center. His breathing stopped. He was dead. That is what happened that Saturday morning.

I did not pursue this question any further. It was too painful for me to ask him about his migraine headache idea. The doctor was not perfect, and he most of all knew that. His friend Walt had come to him with pain, but the answer was too simple, the conclusion quick. He too was human. He was not ready to face up to the fact that this *could* be a tumor, that dreaded, awful diagnosis. He did not want this man of God, with whom he had many a theological discourse, to have anything so devastating.

Some years later I talked with Dr. John Kendig, neurosurgeon, about Walt. He recalled the situation vividly and sadly. He said he was called in on the case that Friday evening. He released the pressure on the swollen brain, but the damage to the brain and body was already done. There was no reversing the deprived brain of oxygen nor hope of survival.

Yes, he could have operated had he been consulted sooner and removed the tumor in the third ventricle of the brain.

I would comfort myself through my tears many times with the relief that Walt did not have to go through (nor did we) what those patients, and their families were going through in the many "vegetable garden" hospital wards of that day. We had been saved from that daily torment. The pain never quits for those families who have loved ones who don't know them, lying there in another world waiting for death to come. My heart cries out for their sadness and feelings of helplessness.

I can and do truly thank God for His gracious mercy to all of us. He had taken Walt to Himself, and away from us, but He had been kind not to let him suffer long. I do not blame God for taking him away. By accepting that man is not perfect, but God is, my anger and suffering has subsided. God forgives all faults and frailties and to God all praise and glory!

By June of 1964 Concordia Publishing House informed me that the book Walt had worked on so hard was coming off the press. It was completed. His book and words would be held within those pages as a memorial to him. I was so happy and excited about this legacy. He would not be lost forever; this would be an indelible memory of one so loved. Walt dedicated the book to our three sons and myself, an honor I still enjoy. Concordia Publishing House had changed the title of the book from Heirs of the Apostles to The Church of the Catacombs, the latter being a more attractive title for all audiences from teenagers to adults. He wrote it for easy reading by all ages. It reads like the morning newspapers, as the reviewers stated.

In 1964 it was also translated into Japanese by Jun Nishizaka in Tokyo. In recent years, all six books of this Church in History series have been completed by other authors. In addition, Walt was rewriting a manuscript for, and in honor of, his old professor, Dr. Theodore Hoyer. Much to my chagrin, that manuscript was never found among his papers after his death. Even though everything had been gone through with great care, that manuscript disappeared. This was a loss for the Hoyer family. My heart goes out to them yet today. Walt's book is still selling 30 years later. I received requests to review his book, which I did for numerous groups in the years that followed.

That summer of 1964 also went down in history as "Freedom Summer." Blacks had lost any glimmer of hope for equality after President Kennedy was assassinated. "Freedom Riders," as Civil Rights workers were called, (blacks and whites) risked their lives for this just cause. The Southern Leadership Conference was also composed of black and white ministers working together. They did not fear losing their jobs because they were paid by their congregations who supported the cause. This was the way to *live* their religion. There were Prayer Marches in Alabama and Mississippi where turmoil was commonplace. Martin Luther King, this man of God, who was fearless and strong, led thousands of people in these peaceful demonstrations. He believed in non-violence (the Gandhian Way). He felt he had nothing to lose and all to gain: *freedom*. Proverbs 29:18 says, "Where there is no vision, the people perish." We have nothing until we have this vision for justice in our life, this freedom we take so much for granted.

Black churches were being bombed, little children killed; Civil Rights workers were beaten, or assassinated. Some vanished off the face of the earth! The KKK was fighting all the way to keep down this "liberty and justice for all" as we say in our "Pledge of Allegiance." How hypocritical to pledge liberty and justice only for themselves! President Lincoln said in his Gettysburg Address: "It is for us the living to *dedicate ourselves* to the proposition that *all* men are *created equal*." My heart bleeds for those who are not allowed this precious gift of equality which our forefathers promised. The Gospel gives this freedom and commands us to "love one another as I have loved you." How we do fall short of what God and country want for all of us and for what we want for ourselves!

Martin Luther King along with his constant companion, Reverend Ralph Abernathy, and other leaders spent many days in jail after being arrested during peaceful, passive demonstrations. Many men of courage like Medgar Evers and Malcolm X lived and fought for freedom in their own way. They were killed for their belief in justice - that all *people* will be judged by their *conscious behavior*.

Blacks daily met reminders of their rejection because of the color of their skin (many still do today). Martin Luther King wanted blacks and whites to feel a "Somebodiness," as he often put it. He sincerely believed in "liberty and justice for all." His wife Coretta also was living proof of special strength, courage and faith given to her by God. He was guiding them up every high mountain, and through every deep valley. Dr. King said: "I have gone to the mountain... I have seen the Promised Land..." He deeply believed there was hope and freedom for all. In *Amos 5:21* it says: *"Let Justice roll down like waters, and Righteousness like an ever flowing stream."* The Kings *lived* their life for God and for their country.

For his personhood and for living out what he stood for, he received the Nobel Peace Prize in 1964.

In 1967 Thurgood Marshall became the first black on the Supreme Court. He said, "In recognizing the humanity of our fellow beings, we pay *ourselves* the highest tribute." How true!

In the early 50's we were beginning the era of greats like "The Late Show" with Jack Paar followed by Johnny Carson. Carson and his friends, Ed McMahon and Doc Severinsen, would be part of our TV life for the next 30 years. For the record, Jay Leno was chosen to follow Johnny in 1992. "Captain Kangaroo" was a daily show for our children in the 50's and 60's. I believe I enjoyed it as much as my boys. We sat together for an hour five days a week enjoying the antics and positive attitude portrayed. Children's lives were enriched by Captain and Mr. Green Jeans, grown men who understood children, their needs and pleasures. "Shari Lewis with Lamb Chop" and "Mr. Rogers' Neighborhood" were other shows they learned from as children.

My sons enjoyed "Superman" comic books as all young boys. "Superman" had begun in my childhood in 1939, and was still existing for my children growing up in the 1960's. An historical note here - He "died" after *53 years* of entertainment (1992).

Our young TV newspeople like Barbara Walters, Tom Brokaw, Jane Pauley, Dorothy Kilgallen, and Dan Rather broadened our horizons, domestic and foreign. We were learning about different life styles, clothes styles, and hair styles.

Comedians like Bob Hope, Jack Benny, George Burns, Phyllis Diller, Milton Berle, Red Skelton, Dinah Shore, Lucille Ball and Desi Arnez had been around for a while providing us an escape from our guilt ridden and confusing country. "Ozzie and Harriet" had been a must for good clean family entertainment for many years.

"Donahue" began his show in '67, as folks gradually opened up and talked about their own personal feelings and experiences. Of course it was interesting to hear about *real life* experiences on television! However, people in 1967 did not share their deep, dark secrets as they do today! This began a more open means of communication.

Music was always a *big* part of our life. The Beatles were so popular with my sons in the 60's. Gregory, from the time he was three, could lift the arm of the phonograph and would play Beatles records. He was a true fan. The Beatles hit their zenith at that same time, 1964.

Tommy, Andy and Greg often did "the twist," a popular dance in those days. Rock and Roll, with Elvis Presley and Little Richard, continued to be a part of our lives, but I insisted we keep the sound down to protect their young ears. Elvis was the "King" of Rock and Roll, a title sealed forever in our minds. He also had some great love songs which many of us hold dear in our hearts these many years. I believe he was a very sad and lonely person needing a lot of love. The pressure to produce ended in a drug overdose and massive heart attack in 1967.

We always had great next door neighbors. First, there were Resident doctors from Washington University Medical Center, and later, Lee Niceley with her two daughters, Rebecca and Tina, and a son, Mark, my boys' age. A lot of fun and antics kept our kids occupied while we sipped our cups of coffee in the backyard. Lee and I both believed in taking out time to relax and enjoy our children, combined with discussions on what was happening in the world. Lee was also single and felt the need for companionship.

In later years, Lee, as a Social Worker, and I, as an R.N., planned a seminar for Health Care Professionals. It was sponsored by the University of Missouri-St. Louis, and a successful venture, I might add. We attracted an interesting group of people to discuss the best ways for doctors, nurses, social workers, hospital chaplains and administrators to work together as a team to give patients the best care.

Lee later married William Cuthill and moved out to the county in the 70's. They recently retired to Arizona.

Marie Heckmann was another creative and enthusiastic friend. She and her husband the Reverend Robert Heckmann would drive in from the little town of New Melle, Missouri, to shop and use my telephone. They were the proud and busy parents of two sets of twins, two girls, Lois and Mary, and two boys, Robert and Richard, born very close together. Marie and I would take our children to many cultural events for which St. Louis is known, children's concerts and ballets. Sometimes it was just a trip to the library to read, and to select a pile of books for the week. It must have had a favorable influence on our children, because between the two families we raised five professionals, actually five medical doctors. Their fourth child became a Lutheran minister, but he is now attending medical school as a second profession. Later, Bob and Marie moved to the East, when he accepted a call to another parish. Ironically, they now live in the same town, Richmond, Virginia, where my Gregory and his wife Amy live. Bob's church is practically in their backyard. It is a small world, isn't it? As we have gotten older, we have progressively developed a very close and loving relationship. They are some of the kindest people I know.

My special friends, Bob and Lori Duesenberg, built a lovely home in South County around this same time. They were having one baby after another, keeping Lori a very busy young mother. Lynda was born the spring after Walt died, Kirsten followed a year later, and then John nearly two years later. Life was hectic for them, but we held on to our close friendship ties even though we both were very busy. We continued the tradition of attending the St. Louis Symphony together. Our mutual love of the great masters of music and our common bond with the past has kept us close these many years. To add to our enjoyment, in 1968 one of the old fine theatres was transformed into the grand Powell Hall. Our Symphony now has one of the acoustically perfect places for us music lovers to enjoy.

I remained close to many of the "old" Seminary friends during those difficult years of adjusting to the single life. I had not moved very far, and I depended upon them for some continuity of the close family life we had mutually enjoyed. They were very kind to our family and would go out of their way to do special things for my sons.

They invited me to Seminary get-togethers for a period of time, but as I began dating, I felt a sense of pulling away from the "old" life. I was slowly developing other friends, and became less dependent upon the past relationships Walt and I had enjoyed together. This was a difficult adjustment, but I sensed some Seminary friends were pulling away as well. I had a feeling I was now part of the past, since I was no longer anyone's wife. Sometimes I felt anger and rejection when I was excluded from a special event, but I kept it all inside.

What really saved my sanity in the long run were my children. Even though I was "tied down," my mind and body were kept busy by the many activities we enjoyed together. I was determined to continue giving them a variety of educational and recreational experiences as they always had. Maybe that would help ease their loss of a father. I wanted them to love life as I did.

Camp Pioneer on Lake Erie near Buffalo, New York, became a wonderful summer escape for our family. It was an LLL Camp (Lutheran Layman's League) where Christian principles were encouraged, along side recreation and relaxation. It became a must for us between 1965 and 1973. The boys and I looked forward to flying to camp every summer. I worked there as the Camp Nurse to pay our way. We received food and lodging free, plus $10.00 a week for treats. That seemed a nice balance and adequate exchange.

I felt a summer camp would be a good place for my boys to enjoy the great outdoors. They could swim (they all had learned to swim in Dr. Arthur and Miriam Piepkorn's pool), and play ball with children their age. I took pride in knowing how to play a pretty fair game of most sports myself. Also, that contact with adult males as role models for them was a pressing issue for me. I did my best to ensure this would happen. Seminary students working as Program Directors and Camp Counselors were good role models and friends for my sons and me. We were getting our life centered - we had lived through enough pain and sadness.

During those summers I rented my home to Seminary students. They needed a place to live while working to pay tuition money in the fall. This plan worked out quite well, except they were generally poor housekeepers! It would take days to get the house in order again when we returned. Nor was I surprised, when I discovered my nine Beethoven symphony records warped! I was angry, but comforted myself with the knowledge that these were only material things.

My thoughts wandered toward the opposite sex on occasion. How could I date someone else? I would be untrue to Walt. After a year of mourning (as was considered in best taste then), I consented to go on my first date. He was a radio personality. I felt rather uncomfortable and so did he. I only wanted to date the best of professional men. Since I had had the best, that is what I would settle for, I told myself: TV newsman, radio announcer, professor, a seminary student, musician, dancing and fencing teacher.

Several close male friends took me to the best affairs St. Louis had to offer. I dressed well, danced well, and made a fun companion for them. Being taller than some by 6 to 8 inches made it easy for us to be just friends! Looking back, those were fun times. I even took dancing lessons from Stanley down the street. He was a *great* dancer and taught fencing as well. My sons wanted to learn fencing, so we struck up a deal. He would teach them fencing and they in turn would learn to dance and be partners for his "fortnightlys." Stanley was a real taskmaster, but Tommy and Andy didn't seem to mind a whole lot. They liked fencing so were willing to sacrifice something to have this privilege. Greg began to learn by the time he was five! They were also learning "proper" manners, which I figured would help them in the future. The barter system was working well for us.

Looking back, I see vividly the privileges my sons had which many children did not. They had sacrificed a lot without a father, but I was making sure they had males in their lives. These men could not take their father's place, but helped tremendously to fill this void and to do things with them. Our Seminary friends were always there for us as a support, but their presence was also a reminder of what we had lost. The more I associated with other males, the more I felt also separation and loss of Seminary friends and the academic surroundings. "Time heals all wounds," they say; but one never forgets. My sons are a living reminder yet today of this loss. That will not go away.

Although I was very busy, I did not want to give up my nursing career. After some inquiries, I decided to accept a position two days a week on the Adolescent Psychiatric Unit at the State Hospital on Arsenal Street. I liked the challenge years earlier while in nurse's training, and felt the experience would be beneficial in raising my sons. Whatever I could learn about children and about myself was important, I mused. Their physical needs were taken care of, but I was not sure about the emotional ramifications of losses.

This experience at the State Hospital proved to be the best thing I ever did. I considered it a privilege to go through what was called "Sensitivity Training" during this time. All the new nurses and doctors were literally locked in for five days as a part of learning how to solve problems, and express feelings. We learned to assert ourselves, and yet be sensitive to the needs of others. We came to know and love each other for what we were. Learning acceptance of people and things we couldn't change was another agenda of the program. My life has been enriched a hundredfold since that training with other professionals. Nothing benefitted me more for life than those five days. I am so thankful for the opportunity. My folks came to stay with my sons during those days. The hospital was caring and understanding allowing me to take a leave of absence in the summer so I could spend it at Camp Pioneer with my sons.

Being a Camp Nurse every summer made a lasting impression and many good memories for my sons and me. I had clinic hours after each of the meals, and children by the dozens would line up to see me. Many were homesick, and just needed a little TLC. I was good at that.

Greg was usually there with me watching and "assisting" me. By just observing, he was learning and feeling what it was like to be sick. The fact is, one *can* make the hurt feel better, I told him. I was a strong influence, he told me in later years after he became a doctor. Every day he helps someone who is in pain physically or emotionally, he helps himself as well. He has experienced the pain of loss.

Along with my part-time job in psychiatry, caring for my boys, and running the household, I took the time to go to Washington University a couple evenings a week. Feeling a need for more of a balance in my overall education, I continued courses in French, English, Anthropology, and Literature. Maybe I would eventually get a degree in Nursing, but for now I needed to continue my studies in Literature and other Fine Arts.

We spent many weekends with my parents near Jacksonville, Illinois, a few miles from the town of Arenzville. Dad had another country parish there, as he always did. He preferred the peace and quiet of the country, and the farm families who made up his parish. This was what he was used to and had done all his life until his retirement in 1968. Our family liked the quiet, too.

The boys had the wide open spaces to explore. There was fishing in the Illinois River just a short distance down the road. They fished for turtles as well! Andy especially loved those creatures and would bring home one or two. More than once he brought home a snapping turtle, but after a nip or two on the finger he would let it go. That was the beginning of our supplying turtles for St. Louis! Neighbor kids loved to play with them, but many of their creatures got away! They kept the bugs out of our basement, though. Even friends would pick up box turtles for my sons as they would find them wandering across a country road. We added them to our collection. Those weekends with my folks were so special, because I could catch up on writing bills, correspondence and sleep. Sunsets were a special joy. My dear Mother would prepare the meals and watch the boys for me. What a joy and eager helpers they were!

Plays were a special favorite of mine. I attended them and acted in one at the Seminary. Greg was only six when we both tried out for "Camino Real" by Tennessee Williams. We both received parts, and enjoyed spending hours in memorizing and rehearsing. Greg would sit there, watching and drawing pictures for hours, while waiting for his little walk-on part.

There had been a recent loss again in my life. I had dated a seminarian ten years my junior and we had fallen in love. It was unrealistic for me to even imagine this young man being a father to three boys. Traditionally, women were reluctant to date men that much younger, let alone think of marriage! Well, this young man left St. Louis for his vicarage year. We wrote for a while, but the distance between age and location was too much. That was the end of that relationship. Painful as it was, it was the best decision for all of us at that point in time.

During the summer months while at camp, I continued correspondence with family and friends. We kept close contact by exchanging visits during the school year. A trip by car or train to see Grandpa and Grandma Oetting was very special. She was so loving and concerned about our family. Her grandchildren meant the world to her. Grandma spent hours on the back porch glider reading to the boys, playing games, and talking about their Daddy.

While at camp, I would drop a card to the men I was dating just to keep in touch. Donald Brauer was one of them. I've had more fun talking about those cards I used to send. If I hadn't done that, I would probably not be married to Don today. After all, I laugh, these men needed to know if I was still available and when I would return!

Don and I knew each other from childhood days in North Dakota, as I wrote in my previous book. We did not know each other as adults until a phone call from Don in 1960. Walt and I were living in the apartment on San Bonita at the time. I naturally invited my childhood friend for dinner that evening, but guess what? He did not show up. He tells me to this day he doesn't recall the invitation, but anyway, maybe it was not in the scheme of things. Don and Walt never met. This was in God's plan for our future, and it was not supposed to be, I guess.

In the fall of 1966 Don and I met again. That was at Concordia Seminary field house, the same place I had met Walt for the second time, I might add. Did God plan everything to begin there?... Don tells everyone he "spotted this beautiful blonde across the crowded room" during a basketball game and discovered it was I. Now this gentleman, Don, was a 34 year old bachelor. (I was a 35 year old widow.) He was obviously keeping his eyes open for a good woman. He wanted to be married by 35, he said years later, or he would give it up as a lost cause.

Don was the youngest of five sons and the only unmarried one of the Reverend Fred and Wanda Brauer. They cherished this last son, believe me. He was single, available, and *wanted* to get married. Wanda was not eager to lose all her sons to other women and certainly not to a woman with three kids, even though we were friends back in North Dakota! Now, I liked the Brauers a whole lot, and thought they were the greatest. They had lived in that big city of Minot in North Dakota, and we used to drive in from the country 50 miles (on a gravel road) just to shop and see them. That was a real special day. Our families had developed close ties during the 30's and 40's. I had known these good folks for many years!

Well, Don walked across the crowded room that night and introduced himself. What a pleasant surprise! We had a great time chatting during the ball game, I can assure you. He was with his brother Paul and his wife Lois, and another teacher friend, Paul Cristler. Great! Here were friends from my childhood past. I was excited, and eager to renew acquaintances.

Don was a good looking fellow, I thought, nicely built with light brown hair, about 5'10", a deep sexy voice - Hmm - nice features - good lips and teeth - and a great cleft chin... Appealing and fun to be with, I thought. I invited them all over to my house after the ball game. Did Don like good classical music? Yes! He admired the nearly 500 albums Walt and I had collected. That common bond was exciting for both of us. Our interests were similar, plus we were both raised in a Lutheran parsonage. Our Dads and Moms knew each other well and had the parish ministry in common. Well, I had to be careful; this was too good to be true, I mused. Here was this terrific man with a nice personality and available -- Wow! Could he be the man for me? Did he like kids? All these questions went through my mind. Maybe he would make a good father for my boys. He sure seemed like the type, I speculated. I better not get my hopes up. That evening was a very happy one. He said nothing about calling me, but that did not matter for I was busy and dating.

Don's folks lived in Hardin, Illinois, where his Dad was the pastor. We did have the opportunity to get together again that fall. Don brought his folks to my parents' home near Arenzville, Illinois, for an anniversary celebration of my Dad's church. His folks may have wanted to look over my sons - who knows? That was a great opportunity, I thought. As I recall, they did not stay long, but it gave Don and me another chance to check each other out. We had a nice chat anyway and then they left.

Sometime during that fall, we stopped in at Don's folks' one late afternoon, purposely taking the long way home from my folks via Hardin. It was quite natural for us to visit someone spontaneously, as our folks did many times in North Dakota. I had called in advance to see if they were going to be home, and was *especially* happy to see Don was there. His Mom invited us to stay for supper. My boys were on their *best behavior*, having been reminded by me that this would be the proper thing to do! They were curiously interested in this new man. Later that evening, I casually told Don I was tired of going out with strange men, and asked if he would consider escorting me to the New Year's Eve party at a friend's home. We could have a good time as "old" friends, I added. He told me yes. Wow! Nothing like arranging my own dates! I thought that was quite bold of me, but then I figured this guy might need a bulldozer to get him off dead center! I sensed his Mom would be pulling the other direction, and I could not blame her a bit. Being a Mom, I understand even more fully today how much you would like to have one son remain "faithful," so to speak, and stay close to you.

New Year's Eve came. We were invited for the party at my lovely, old home on Alamo, where Professor Andrew and Wilma Weyermann now lived. Can you imagine taking your date to your previous home! I surely had nerve, but then we were old friends, I said to myself. Andy and Wilma had moved in two years ago from North Carolina where Andy had been a parish pastor. We had known each other from student days at the Seminary (they were like Walt and I, married in their last year at the Seminary) and now were my neighbors. Small world! Wilma was a special friend, a lot of fun and laughter when she was around. (She died tragically of a brain tumor some years later.) Professor Norman and Barbara Habel were close friends just down the street, who had come from Australia. Barbara too was a joy to be with and helped lighten up sad times. (They returned to their homeland in the 70's.) We were together for parties on special occasions in each other's homes. Pool parties at Professor Don and Corinne Deffner's were another highlight in our life. They welcomed and shared their blessings with so many of us!

My sons and I kept up the tradition of having an open house around Christmas each year. We enjoyed company so much, and they were eager helpers in taking people's coats and making conversation with many friends from the Seminary. They were used to being around educated men and women, which I felt was a good influence for them.

Well, all my Seminary friends met Don that evening at Weyermanns, and they liked him. I was so pleased that they were willing to accept seeing me with someone other than Walt. I was not sure they would, as there were folks who still had not totally accepted Walt's death. There may have been some thinking that I should not get interested in another man. After all, I had the best, so why be "unfaithful" to my dead husband and, who knows, down deep, I most likely had that same feeling. I was working through it, however sad it made me feel. I had been in counseling which was most helpful. Now nearly three years later I needed to get on with my life, and pursue what was best for my sons and me.

Don and I just talked and laughed all evening, till the early hours of the morning. We hit it off beautifully and seemed to be on the same wave length. The champagne helped, too! We felt so comfortable together because of our close ties from the past. He told me he dated but never found the right person to marry. He was currently in a Master's program at Southern Illinois University, Edwardsville, Illinois. An M.A. degree in Music Education, which he was concentrating on at this time, was important to him. He had recently returned from New York City, where he had a good job with TWA Airlines. He said he was tired of that hectic life and liked being back in the Midwest.

Don had graduated as valedictorian of his high school class in the tiny town of Monango, North Dakota, in 1951. He came to the big city (as I had done) to enroll at Concordia University, River Forest, a Lutheran institution in that suburb of Chicago. He planned to become a teacher. After receiving his B.A. degree there in 1956, he taught parochial school for several years. Don felt unfulfilled, he said. He worked at Stix, Baer & Fuller Department Store for a period of time, and then later became a Reservationist with TWA.

He enjoyed taking his folks to Europe one summer, as he could get inexpensive rates while working for the airlines. The following year, he made a trip around the world *by himself*. Wow! This man was *independent*, I found out, and I would be reminded of that fact many times in the next 25 years!

As a person who was *used* to living alone, Don was comfortable in that life style. How could I imagine in my fondest dreams that he could be shaken loose to marry a woman with three children. Never in a million years!

Even though I was a busy woman caring for my sons, and had a full life, I did not feel complete without a man in the house. I could handle everything fine, but there was this void - I needed a *husband*, and my sons needed a *father*. I felt this was so important for their future emotional welfare. Don't get me wrong, my male friends were especially nice to my sons and took an interest in giving them extra attention. That father image to model after was missing.

I had treated myself to a grand three week trip to Europe in 1966 before leaving for Camp in New York. The Concordia Cantata Chorus and Orchestra, under the direction of Professor Robert Bergt and accompanied by his good wife Joan, toured Europe giving wonderful concerts to packed audiences. They were an accomplished group of musicians which I considered a privilege to know. My Mom and Dad had taken the boys to the country for those weeks I was gone. They were always there for me, never reluctant to lend me a helping hand. Besides, the boys liked being out in the country, fishing, and having the freedom of running around in the open spaces.

After that splendid New Years' Eve together I did not hear from Don again until he responded to the postcard I sent him the summer of 1967. I was at Camp Pioneer with my sons, as I previously said, and keeping in touch with my friends and family was of utmost importance to me.

After we returned from camp, Don called me in late August and asked me out for dinner. Well, you can imagine that got me excited all over again! The reason he did not call for a year, as I found out later, was that he was *dating* another woman, besides completing his Master's degree. That fall we began dating about once a week. He would pick me up in his old 1960 blue Volkswagen Bug. A blanket was kept in the car for the cold months as his heater wasn't working! I figured he planned to get a new car eventually, so he didn't want to throw money into an old vehicle. Practical man he was! He was used to having little money, scrimping with little left over to save. That was the way he was raised, and the way Walt and I were raised. That was the way of a preacher's family.

We liked each other's company a lot. My sons liked him and got along fine with him. Don loved to laugh and play games with us. We were all falling in love together. Don was *our man*. However, unabashed joy would not be ours. It would be just a few short months before I felt our world was falling into a deep hole.

BACH GAVE US GOD'S WORD

MOZART GAVE US GOD'S LAUGHTER

BEETHOVEN GAVE US GOD'S FIRE

GOD GAVE US MUSIC THAT

WE MIGHT PRAY WITHOUT WORDS

From a German Opera House

CHAPTER SIX

THE LATE 1960'S
ASSASSINATIONS OF DR. MARTIN LUTHER KING
AND
ROBERT F. KENNEDY
REBELLION AND CHAOS IN THE COUNTRY
AND AT HOME

"Free at Last
Free at Last
Thank God Almighty
I'm Free at Last..."

Dr. Martin Luther King

"I have fought a good fight,
I have finished my course
I have kept the faith..."

2 Timothy 4:7

Our lives, as well as those of the whole country and world, were shaken to the core once again. On April 4, 1968 the life of Dr. Martin Luther King was snuffed out by a single assassin's bullet. He would not live to see freedom for all, nor to see equality and justice for his people. James Earl Ray shot the gun that killed this great warrior at the Lorraine Motel in Memphis, Tennessee. At age 39, another young man had been assassinated

Just the day before Dr. King had delivered his "I've Been to the Mountaintop" speech in Memphis. These would be his last words to a large crowd. He was also preparing for the "Poor People's Campaign" with a march on Washington D.C., planned for April. My mind can only think of the great shock and sadness our country expressed, when we heard he was killed. A jarring of the body like a tremendous earthquake was followed by a volley of despair, with floods of tears rolling over our nation like a tidal wave. I remember that day as if it were yesterday.

Over these years my mind has stopped many times, just reacting to that moment in time; my heart is heavy and my eyes fill with tears as I write these words 25 years later. This was a tremendous blow to our nation. We had gathered up hope again after the deadly shot that killed our President just four years earlier. It was much too soon for me after my husband's death. Four years is not enough time to recover - the heart cannot suffer such blows - the losses were too soon and too many. The world mourned...

After that week of despair, the anger from all the years of repression exploded like a bolt of lightning. Everything was in chaos in our country. The people had finally said "No more. We have had enough of this injustice in our lifetime!" Surprisingly, there was not a lot of violence directed toward people, but toward property, with burning and looting of stores occurring in many cities. Washington D.C. and Detroit were hit the hardest with days of pillaging. Our country in all 50 states was on fire with rage, and the buildings with it. Thousands of people were injured, left homeless, and millions of dollars worth of property damaged. Dr. King's widow, Coretta, still insisted that non-violence was the best way. Her husband had been willing to die for the cause of peace and nonviolence, and his memory and his work would be lost forever if the people's anger were to come out in acts of fury. National Guardsmen and state troopers were out on the streets of many cities as strikes took place in numerous industries. The mayors gave orders to shoot to kill looters and arsonists. Jesse Jackson was quoted as saying they might have a program to kill dreamers, but not dreams. Hundreds of protestors were in jail. It was worth all trials, this fight for justice. And it is worth the dream... Dr. King's "I Have a Dream" speech was delivered so long ago it seemed (August 1963).

America's conscience was being tugged. When would justice come? We had a pluralistic society, but little equality was being insisted upon for all its members. It had only been three years previously that the Voting Rights Act was signed by President Johnson.

My thoughts travel to this passage on the day of Dr. King's funeral: "Greater love hath no man than this, that he lay down his life for his brother," John 15:13. It was reported that on April 9, 1968, 150,000 persons attended Dr. King's funeral, the largest funeral ever given a private citizen.

President Johnson, along with senators, governors, and mayors from around the country, and members of all races, religions, and walks of life attended his funeral. Everyone was devastated. Television showed every moment. Robert Kennedy, Dr. King's trusted friend, marched and sang with the crowd during a five-mile stretch of road that day in Atlanta. Jacqueline Kennedy, widow of President John F. Kennedy, with her courage and presence gave strength to Mrs. King in this hour of need.

One month later, Coretta King herself led the march on Washington D.C. for the Poor People's Campaign. Dr. King's work would continue; his loyalty to this just cause was not lost. "We shall overcome..." rang through the streets. This song of the nonviolent movement spread through many of our hurting cities as blacks and whites sang it together over and over again. Surely, "let freedom ring..."

Life was a roller coaster of emotions for me. Don and I were in love, and yet there seemed again so little love left in those angry streets. My life was full with caring for my family and keeping things together. I hurt for my sons too, for the fear and insecurity within their souls. Would they always be taken care of by Mommy? They knew the strife going on, but did not know how to deal with it. There was a need to be reassured time and time again. That was foremost in my mind at every word and action I took. "I will always be there for them," I said. Don and I took them with us many times when we went out. More and more of our dates were family dates.

Late spring of that year we were invited by friends to visit their farm. It was a lovely, sunny day which I vividly recall. We had so much fun seeing all the animals, riding whatever there was to ride, and walking in the field away from the big, sad city. Don and the boys were hitting it off so well.

On the ride back home that night, while my sons were sleeping soundly, Don asked me to marry him. It seemed the natural thing to do, and I was comfortable with the thought of being his wife. We loved each other very much; Don's relationship with my sons and theirs with him was good. If they had reservations about it, none was expressed.

We told the boys about our engagement the next afternoon. They were happy and excited. The prospect of a new father was something to look forward to with great anticipation. My concern of course was whether things would work out. Would the boys always care for Don? Would they reject him in later years? How would Don treat my sons after we were married? I had many questions and fears, but Don and I were prepared to face them together with God's help. We all had a strong faith in God who had brought us through deep sadness. Now the five of us would have joy together - this was our hope.

Don and I picked out rings one afternoon in May. He wanted the best diamond he could afford for his bride-to-be. We selected a solitaire, the size of diamond I could not even imagine wearing. When they say "diamonds are a girl's best friend," that may be partially true. It was gorgeous; it was big! I couldn't believe he wanted this for me. I wore the modest size diamond ring from Walt on my right hand. (It was later stolen.) Oh, I said to myself, I had been through a lot and deserved this lovely ring. I was thrilled then, but even more so on the evening he finally gave me the ring after it was sized. It was June 5th. The place? Neither of us can remember...!

I was so excited, I wanted to show it off to my friends. I do not recall my sons' reactions, but I know they were happy. This ring sealed our love; our future life together was assured, and my boys would have a father.

Friends stopped by that next day to see my ring. They knew we were planning to get married eventually, but this was the clincher. This brave and courageous man had taken an important step toward marrying a woman with three kids! He had to be special - and to give her a big ring - well, he was some kind of super guy!

My living room was cluttered with unfinished ladder-back chairs, which I was antiquing a familiar green (the "in" thing that year). I had purchased them at Famous Barr Department Store at two for $15.00, a neat bargain!

Months earlier I had been fortunate to get the bid at a farm auction for a lovely antique oak table. It had lion's paw feet, and came with five boards, just what I wanted. I was so excited about my purchase - to have out-bid two other bidders who were males was more than I could fathom. When the bidding took place my last bid was $52.50. There was dead silence... What happened to those guys? Why weren't they bidding? I couldn't believe it... I had the last bid! My knees were shaking, my face flushed with excitement. My hands shook so much I could hardly write the check for the purchase. Now, I finally had a large dining room table where everyone could sit together. It would seat fourteen in a pinch, I figured.

My faithful father had my table delivered to their home out in the country near Arenzville, Illinois. He wanted to remove the old varnish of many years. I had to be back in St. Louis the next morning. Strange how things happen; two days earlier I had offered $100.00 for that same table, but they refused, figuring they could get more for it than that. "All things come to those who wait." How true! I learned another lesson that day.

About a month later Mom and Dad came to visit us and guess what? They had the table with them. Dad had spent hours removing the old dark varnish from years of preserving, and it was ready for refinishing. How happy and moved I was. He and Mom were that way, just doing special things to help and never asking for a thank you. I don't believe we ever thank our parents enough for all those little things. How much we take for granted! I know I did.

As I look back on the years and remember as they were getting old, I *did* help them out a lot, and tried to be there for them. I feel good about that now. The boys did take things for granted when they were young too, so it must be in the natural scheme of things. I have great hope that Gregory will be there for me when I am old. He appears to be the most sensitive of my sons.

Anyway, that old table was then sanded and refinished by me, with the help of a hired seminary student. We polished it till it shone. That masterpiece is in my dining room today. It now stands as a symbol of a lot of love, hard work, and many memories of family and friends and delicious meals. It symbolizes the happiest of times - every occasion special to me, every memory cherished. Pictures were *always* taken around it. The memory of those times around my table are preserved, never to be forgotten. This table will be an heirloom for my son, Gregory. He will have it in his dining room one day, with as much joy for his family, and he will pass it down to his son, Reid Walter. Who knows, maybe he too will pass on this story of my special long awaited dining room table.

Back to that day when friends were stopping by to congratulate me. It was June 6, 1968. The radio was playing some great classical music as usual, when suddenly it was interrupted by a news flash. Shots had rung out one more time. Robert Francis Kennedy, the 42-year-old younger brother of John Fitzgerald Kennedy, lay fatally wounded in Los Angeles. He had just finished a campaign speech while running for the presidency of the United States. He had been shot in the head as he was leaving. He was not expected to live.

A man named Sirhan Sirhan had vented his rage on the man he thought was his problem. This fragile-looking Arab was blaming Robert Kennedy for the United States' support of Israel, and for the Arabs' defeat. I could not believe it, I did not want to believe it. *This was more than I was going to accept!* How could such terrible things happen again and again? Was our world going totally crazy? Would there never be an end to it, I cried! My heart was torn into pieces that day - this was the end of hope for peace and justice for me and for so many in our country. It was a personal thing for me: It was like putting "all your eggs in one basket" (as the saying goes) but the basket kept tipping over, breaking all the eggs.

Robert Kennedy was our last hope for an open society with equal opportunity for blacks and minorities. He could finally alleviate the guilt carried by the white man for years of slave-holding. He could bring rich and poor together. Could we finally "love our neighbor as ourselves" as it says in Matthew 22? Ending the war in Vietnam was a promise he would fulfill. He was dedicated to equality, and carried on this banner of hope for John F. Kennedy and Martin Luther King. He was running for the presidency to fulfill this dream for us. He had just won the California primaries after several successive wins in other states. Jubilation was short for him that day in the Ambassador Hotel in Los Angeles; the violence he wanted to end *ended* with his own violent death.

In shock and desperate for comfort, I called Don out of his classroom that day. In tears, I needed to tell him right away what had happened. He too, could not believe such sad news. How unfair it was that our great joy was dampened by such sorrows The tears seemed never to cease completely since that day. There remains an aura of sadness and hopelessness grasping at the heart of our nation. Our country lost its direction one last time, and we have never again had a leader who could clear the narrow path to freedom for all. Bringing blacks and whites together for a common goal is yet a dream, a hopeless wish for many others.

My sons experienced this sadness with us. They were so young and fragile emotionally. At 12, 11, and 7 they had swallowed a lot of bitter pills. How would they ever grow up to be healthy and whole people? Would not all this turmoil and these deaths affect their lives in terrible ways? Little did I know how it would affect them as their lives unfolded...

I tried to protect them from the impact these numerous sad events had on my life. But it was hard to suppress the tears that would come, tears of supreme sadness and frustration. I wept, too, for all those widows and fatherless children, not only in the Kennedy and King families, but for the families of all those who died in the Civil Rights movement. What would ever happen to them? Nothing could fill the hole in their lives left by the assassins' bullets. They too were doomed to suffer. Their losses were our losses. In John 14:21 it says "My peace I leave with you... Let not your heart be troubled..." God would have to take care of all these little ones, for we mothers could not do it all alone.

The clash that followed Robert Kennedy's death was the beginning of the end for the peace movement. On the one hand was the political machine of the people attempting to work within our Democratic system. On the other hand were the anti-everything factions working outside the system. These two unrelenting forces met at the National Democratic Convention in Chicago that summer of 1968. Chaos and rebellion were the order of the day.

Hippies, with their wild long hair and beards, marched on the convention hall. I remember vividly from the television coverage the many clashes of these demonstrators with the police and Illinois National Guardsmen. Rocks and anything that could be picked up were thrown. The anger of many youths in their twenties and younger exploded as these forces joined together to express their outrage of these last years of killings and violence. Some were anti-war, some anti-establishment (that meant against everything from the past), some anti-Christ, and some were all three. They vented their anger toward the police and toward property, with the result that many were injured and many jailed. The cause for peace and justice was all but forgotten.

There were many of us right in the middle of both sides, a terrible situation to be in! It was not clear who was for whom except that just about *everyone* was against *someone*. We knew that for sure from the newspapers, radio, and television coverage. The mildest thing I can say about those chaotic months and the decade that followed was that it was *wild*.

I did not like what I was *seeing* or what I was *hearing* Rebellion was shown in the abuse of drugs of all kinds being ingested, smoked, or sniffed. Every good parent worried to death! The shock of drug abuse personally came to my knowledge when I was the nurse at Camp Pioneer. I saw the change coming through the teenagers who came those following summers. It was unreal to hear a child of *nine* tell how he "best got a buzz" by taking Darvon capsules apart and swallowing the tiny pink pill inside. (They no longer make them that way.) I proceeded to ask how he found out about this and he said his mother worked in a pharmacy, and she told him! Another youth told me how their friends had parties to share drugs. They would steal the pills from their medicine chests at home, toss them together like salad, then the bowl was passed around, each one taking as many pills as they wanted to ingest at one time! It was strictly a game of chance, live or die - no one knew what the pills were for; no one cared, except they wanted to appear brave - it was the defiant thing to do.

The young people became increasingly difficult to handle. They were rebelling against anyone and everyone. Parents, a symbol of authority and responsibility, were "out." "Let it all hang out" was the cry. To show love toward your parents was a definite no-no. I had children coming to me in my clinic crying, because they really "did not want to be against their parents!" But they didn't want to be unpopular either.

Hip–hugger jeans with bell bottoms dragging on the ground was the dress of the day; the hair was long or Afro, unkempt, and the body *occasionally* washed. Fleas in the body hair were common, being passed from one person to another through a promiscuous sex life. How was I as a nurse to keep the infections down when these young people were living in such a manner that "anything goes?" There were no parameters. Many would not *take* responsibility for *their* behavior. There was not total agreement among them regarding this life style, but those who did not agree dared not speak up. It seemed many were obliged to go along with the crowd, although privately they would come to me as the nurse telling in tears how they were *really* thinking and feeling. What were they to do? My suggestion was to follow what they knew to be right and responsible, but I really wondered who would have the *courage* to stand up against this *mass* of wayward youth who appeared to be out of control.

It is so difficult for me to put into words that adequately describe the attitude and behavior of that generation of youth. *It is like* your *worst dream*. Looking back on it, I actually feel ill. It is a nightmare I want to forget, but can't, at least not until I have expressed the feelings I still harbor. Many parents still carry in their hearts and minds the fears and hurts by their children during that era.

I felt the frustration of being in the position of a nurse at camp and trying to help the teens there (including my own), and later as campus nurse for the college crowd at Washington University. I truly felt things were out of hand. It was hopeless. "The Dawning of the Age of Aquarius" was here. The music of the Beatles and Rock bands reflected the mass rebellion: confusion, compounded by the use of drugs. Free love and free use of drugs of all kinds were encouraged by their peers. The louder the music the better.

Already in 1967 "Woodstock" had brought together every young person who followed the crowd. With clothes off, minds floating, they made love and had free sex. These psychic "acts" or whatever they were called, were to symbolize freedom. Peace symbols were everywhere. They truly did want peace as we all did; however, the formula was not correct. Physical freedom without any responsibility equals no peace.

The traditional family with mother, father and children was breaking down. Dissension and heartbreak in the family were common. My generation was taught to be responsible for our own behavior and attire, while our children were rejecting everything that we wanted to pass on to them. Why were we supposed to change our way of thinking?

It became quite clear to me that this totally "free" behavior was, foremost, *harmful* and the use and abuse of drugs destroyed many young minds. I was aware of friends' children and young people on campus and off campus - in communes - who ended up on the psychiatric wards in hospitals; others committed suicide. The abuse caused distorted thinking and enabled many young persons to put an end to their lives before life had barely begun for them. This was the saddest result of it all.

Families were torn apart by what they viewed as "right" and "responsible." Parents disagreed and each went their own way, beginning an era of divorce. It used to be that families would stick together through "thick and thin." We followed our marriage vows "to love one another until death parted us." Now it was common to love one another until someone else came along who might be a better lover. We were in shock hearing of friends' marriages breaking up. A majority of Don's and my families stuck it out together, riding the waves, rough as they were. Their faith in God remained strong. In John 14:27 it says, "My peace I leave with you. Let not your heart be troubled. Let it not be afraid." There is also a saying that success in marriage is much more than *finding* the right person; it is a matter of being the right person.

It was the young against the old, the hippie against the squares, the new way of life against the old way. We had a major battle on our hands Sometimes it became fuzzy as to who *we* versus they were. People took sides across all races, religions and ages. Even God was declared dead by many, and signs were made to state that belief!

Despite what was happening in the world, I *worked at maintaining peace* in our home, no matter the odds I was up against. We tried, even though everyone was far from being perfect. Don and I had not been raised perfectly; our folks made mistakes, but we were willing to accept mistakes. If I didn't, how could I ever get over my husband's death? His doctor was not perfect, and we cannot expect that any doctor be perfect. There would be no way I could raise my three sons, I told myself, if I could not accept what I could not change. My spirit and zest for life I vowed never to lose. I *must* make Don's and my upcoming marriage work, or I would die trying...

CHAPTER SEVEN

Marriage To Don
Turmoil In The Early 1970's
Working For Justice And Peace
Mother Oetting's Death

"Love Me, That's All I Ask of You..."

Add to Your Faith Virtue;
And to Your Virtue, Knowledge;
And to Knowledge, Temperance;
And to Temperance, Patience;
And to Patience, Godliness;
And to Godliness, Brotherly Kindness;
And to Brotherly Kindness, Charity..."

2 Peter 3:5–8

It was August 31, 1968, and a beautiful day dawned for Don's and my wedding. Even though the world was in turmoil, we were bringing our families together. My little family of three growing, active sons, Tom, Andy and Greg, would be knit together with our love. We would be merged and become the Oetting–Brauer family. What an exciting time for all of us!

Many of our three families and friends came together that day at Bethel Lutheran Church, Clayton, in St. Louis, also the location of the school my sons attended. They filled the church. Our fathers and Don's oldest brother, Hank, participated in our beautiful worship service of joy. I knew him well from years ago in North Dakota. He was a great preacher, and always tried to make his sermons relevant for the times. He had a great sermon on "loving one another" that day. Shortly thereafter he resigned from his congregation in New York. He told us later the people in his congregation did not wish to hear about happenings in our society that were relevant to their daily lives.

A marriage litany was written by Reverend Steve Albers. He was the Program Director at Camp Pioneer in New York that summer, and wanted to do this very special thing just for Don's and my wedding. It was beautiful.

Numerous family members who were in the music field enhanced our wedding with their talents. The mutual love of music was intertwined among our families. My brother Bob played the organ and Don's twin brothers, Paul and Fritz, sang and played the violin (consecutively). Fritz and Bob were musicians and professors at Concordia College in St. Paul, Minnesota, and Paul was a school principal in St. Louis. Fritz's son, Fred, was the trumpeter. My three sons were actively taking lessons with piano (Tom), violin (Greg), and trumpet (Andy), but were still in the learning stages, and not perfected for a wedding. They took an active part with Tom as the acolyte, Andy the marriage banner–bearer, and Gregory the ring bearer. I sensed a great pride in each of them taking part as a family member.

Between all the pastors and musicians in our families, the knot was well tied. Don and I were bound together forever, we hoped. In our wedding bands is engraved I John 4:18, which says, "There is no fear in love, but perfect love casts out fear. For fear has to do with punishment, and he who fears is not perfected in love. We love, because He first loved us."

My sons were excited, because they would have a man in their life to be a model for them. They too would have a father, like most of their friends. Even though there had been numerous men involved in our lives, this was different. He would be their *father* and that was *very* important to them. That was equally important to me. We could not praise God enough for this special gift of Don to our family!

Don continued to teach music to the young ones across the river in Roxana and Wood River, Illinois, after we were married. At this writing, he has served over 25 years in that school district, and was recently recognized for this accomplishment. He also became the organist at a Lutheran Church, Chapel of the Cross in north St. Louis County. He held that position for seven years. Our lives continued to be surrounded by good music. Don joined Bob, Lori and me regularly at the Symphony.

Society in general was revolving around Rock and Roll. The louder the music, the better seemed to be the trend in the late 60's and 70's. My sons had been exposed to a variety of good music before this wave of rebellion in music hit. They never did insist upon turning the volume up to ear–deafening heights; however, many parents did have this problem. We were all fearful these children could eventually lose their hearing.

After Don and I were married, we moved into the very first home either of us owned. A lovely, all brick ranch style home at 4425 Crestland Drive, Northwoods, a suburb of St. Louis, in the Normandy School District. It was in a neighborhood that was "changing," a word that we would hear *forever*, as if it were a bad word, a word to be whispered around like some evil lurking in the shadows. It was not a familiar word or action so to us it was okay. After all, we had made many "changes" and adjustments in our lives. We knew we could handle changes, and if it were changes in color or race, that was fine with us. God had guided our footsteps all the way and it was all up to Him.

Little did we know that a lot of folks did not look at our changing neighborhood the same way. "For sale" signs sprung up around our home and in the neighborhood like flowers that spring. We were quite amazed and appalled! What was going on? What was happening? Who could tell us? When we would ask these neighbors with "for sale" signs on their lawns, they would make desperate statements of anxiety about "the colored" moving in.

I have never ceased to wonder about those folks. What was so wrong with blacks moving in, and, why was the color of folks still so important? Weren't we ever just going to care for each other as people? That is where I was, anyway. In 1 John 4:11–12, it says, "If God so loved us, we also ought to love one another. No man has ever seen God; if we love one another, God abides in us and His love is perfected in us." I came across another gem of wisdom about our humanness just the other day: "Still lost in a crowd of their kind, man turns away from a plurality which disturbs them."

As we saw new neighbors around us, I made it a point to welcome them. Some were even surprised, and if they were, I was happy to be the surpriser.

Within the first year, we were considered the "old neighborhood," as there were so many new people. In Galatians 3:28 it says "we are one in Christ." That we tried to be.

I never ceased to wonder about the many people who seemed to disappear into the night, and others who appeared just as suddenly in their place. Now, I can tell you, when that happened so quickly with the four homes in front of our long front lot, it was a shocker! We did pause for a moment to reflect, and to wonder about the meaning of all of this, and when it would end. After all, it was a new and strange phenomenon, this disappearance of folks. Where were they going and from what were they running? We were to discover from rumors that South, West and St. Charles counties were havens for white folks. Well, at least they thought so anyway. (That was 25 years ago.)

Where was this peace and justice that Martin Luther King Jr. was talking about? Weren't we to be the instruments of God to bring about justice and equality in our world? In Matthew 5:9, it says: "Blessed are the peacemakers, for they shall be called the children of God."

By that next year I made a special sign. I did it with great care, because I wanted it to last a *long* time. It was a 20" x 35" banner made of red felt with the words printed in white felt: *"Peace Among All Men."* This, I nailed to our front door for everyone to see. I wanted all who drove by, or who came to see us, to know what I felt about the *integration* of people. There would be *no doubt* in our new neighbors' minds, or in anyone's mind how we felt.

It is said that racism is as deadly as a gun. It kills the spirit, it destroys the body just as a disease. It kills trust between the races, because we know no freedom as long as we are bound by racism. Joseph Barndt wrote about this in his book Liberating Our White Ghetto way back in the early 1970's. Dismantling Racism is his recent publication, which I highly recommend.

I must tell you, I remade that banner several times over, these many years; but now I have hanging by the door, a peace wreath, which my son Greg and his wife Amy gave us. They know how we feel. Thank God for them. If there is anyone left who doubts how I feel about a peaceful, integrated neighborhood it isn't my fault! Without freedom to love each other, we cannot see the gift from God we are to each other. We got deeply involved in keeping peace in our changing neighborhood, but I will talk about that later.

That November, 1968, the "Silent Majority" elected Richard M. Nixon for President, and we began another era. A quiet, sinister, underhanded revolt began against those who were not *for* or *part of* the establishment.

Each of us in our new family were unique individuals, and as diverse as our multi–cultural neighborhood. We also had all ends of the genetic spectrum under our roof, I believe. Greg and I had some of the same genetic makeup, and Tom and Andy shared some of the same genes, as they had the same mother and father. Don had his own set of genes. This was definitely a challenge to bring us all together into a strong working family!

Well, it was more *idealistic* than *realistic* to think things would run smoothly in our household — it didn't. I found myself immediately cast into the role of communicator, mediator, and peacemaker. I had no choice. I was bound by conscience, as I had brought us all together. (God receives a lot of credit, too.) I felt it was necessary for *each* to carry his own load of responsibility for his behavior, as a peaceful contributor to the family. Well, most of us parents know what happens to that great "idea" (I'll call it) when one has teenagers.

Tom and Andy were now teenagers, and they wanted "to do *their own thing,*" (as it was "in vogue" to do) and in *their own time*. They were wanting to have a new Dad, but did not want to put out the necessary effort to get to know this Dad. Well, one can only want something for someone else so long, and then someone pays the price. Tom and Andy were the losers. You see, when it came down to it, each of us as individuals must work on our self–esteem to reach the point of maturity where we feel good about ourselves. They did not. There is a quote saying: "We are what our thoughts make us," which was so poignant in our family. Also, bonding did not take place for Andy and Tommy as babies. They now refer to it as an "attachment disorder." The acceptance of love, and responsibility for actions is absent. Bonding with Greg and myself took place when he was born. Tommy and Andy were remembering all the losses and disappointments in their young lives, and these were like yesterday to them.

Tom led the way to rebellious behavior, and Andy followed. The scenario goes like this: grades start spiralling downward, Mom or Dad remind them of the consequences of poor grades (no extracurricular activities like sports or television). They insist upon it anyway, until they are caught. Frantic yelling sessions occur, followed by leaving the house and slamming the door behind. Sound familiar?

I finally declared there would not be an evening dinner until we as a family sat down together and talked things out that were bothering them that day. Usually this was in the living room. Each would have the opportunity to share his feelings, and what was going on in his life. Nice idea, but not everyone wanted to share. Some wanted to keep their own thoughts and angry feelings to themselves. They had nothing to say. That was part of *power* and they were in control of it. Expressing themselves in passive aggressive behavior became the norm for Tommy and Andy.

So now what do you do? My peace plan for everyone was not working. Well, how can we change negative thoughts of one's self into positive ones? I recalled this timely quote by Eleanor Roosevelt: "Remember, *no one* can make you *feel inferior* without your consent." All the positive things like love, food, clothing, Mom, Dad, brothers, money, God, communication, praise for a job well done were not working. All the negative things were foremost in our minds.

Don came across this bit of humor one day: "We the willing, led by the unknowing, are doing the impossible for the ungrateful. We have done so much for so long, with so little, we are now qualified to do anything with nothing!"

The arguments and disagreements were spiralling downward toward a no–win situation for all of us. They say that discussion is an exchange of knowledge; argument is an exchange of ignorance. Wisdom is knowing what to do with what we know. I was at a loss as to what to do with what I knew, but was not willing to give up. Failure is endeavor, and endeavor persisted in, is not failure, I reminded myself from pages in my Psychology book, so we persisted in trying to work out each difficult situation.

Tommy and Andy were 13 and 12, and Gregory was seven when Don and I were married. Greg was thinking about becoming a doctor already. From little on he worked hard and enthusiastically at whatever he did. He had this plan and he persisted in preparing himself to become what he wanted to be.

It was not easy without a father for any of my sons in those very early years. Later, adjusting to a "new" father was difficult. When Greg saw the behavior of his two older brothers it was upsetting for him as well. Some days were spent addressing the needs and problems of the moment.

We worked at the positive things. Gregory became the same way. He too had a fear of becoming like his older brothers, so he kept his mind occupied doing whatever he did well. He enjoyed taking the Suzuki method of learning the violin. With Don accompanying on the piano, he practiced for upcoming concerts with the other Suzuki players. Dr. John Kendall, who became Greg's teacher, had brought this method over from Japan. (He was and still is a professor at Southern Illinois University, Edwardsville.) What a thrill that this master consented to teach our son!

Beginning at eight years of age, Greg played in concerts with as many as 100 aspiring little violinists. We were so proud of him! His drive to succeed was *enormous*. He had the will to do what he wanted, and would rise above the difficulties at every turn. Nothing seemed to stop him. No matter how hard it was, he wanted to master it. He was going toward one of his goals, and that was to master the violin.

I thank God every day for my special gift from God of this son who was so talented. The *drive* and the *will* to persist and "*do* what he had to do" came from both Walt and me. It was in his genes. Gregory was truly blessed, as we used to say about each other. Walt would not see the end result of such a gifted child, but he knew his Gregory was someone very special. Gregory knew it as well. His self–esteem was there. One only has to look at the two pictures of Greg and his biological Dad that hang on our walls to know — it is in the eyes, the smile, the touch —*therein is love*. These pictures are in the middle of the book. What more does a young child need, but to understand, to accept and to feel love?

We have given Gregory the continued hugs, encouragement and praise over these many years, carrying on what God gave us, His love in our child. My feeling is strong on this continuation of our expressions of love.

> In the 70's the Surgeon General had determined that hugging was good for our health.
>
> Hugging is practically perfect: No movable parts, no batteries to wear out, no periodic check-ups, low energy consumption, high energy yield, inflation-proof, non-fattening, no monthly payments, no insurance requirements, theft-proof, non-taxable, non-polluting, and, of course, fully returnable.
>
> Hugging is all natural: Organic, naturally sweet, no pesticides, no preservatives, no artificial ingredients, 100% wholesome.
>
> The best people, places and times to hug: Anyone, anywhere, anytime.
>
> ...from Self Esteem Seminars

For me, there is no other behavior which expresses how I feel. No other action returned tells me how another person feels toward me. No other activity has brought more tears of relief, of joy, of understanding than a hug. There are those that avoid it or modify it in various ways, but I am undaunted when it comes to hugging!

Interestingly enough I was raised *without* a lot of hugging or displays of affection; but apparently I received enough. I have no particular craving for affection, but I do enjoy giving and receiving hugs.

I came to realize this about affection since being married to Don. The Brauer families have this wonderful quality of displaying affection freely. They do not mind having their feelings known, whether they are good, bad or indifferent. Some of the excitable feelings are not easily understood, but I have learned to laugh with them and accept them. The

“Brauerei” as they often call a large gathering of Brauers, seems to accept this quality of open feelings about each other. They often refer to some over-exerted behavior as “they are just being a Brauer.” I can accept that.

There are many Brauers across this land and in Germany. Reunions have been in Europe every ten years, but just one large one in the United States. Two of the Brauer cousins who are sisters, Evelyn Stieg and Lois Breseman, chaired and coordinated this first great event in 1989. Invitations were sent out by heads of families across this great land. Everybody who was a Brauer, or had married into the family, or was related somewhere along the line, came. A throng of over 400 gathered in River Forest, Illinois, a suburb of Chicago. They shared their lives and their family histories. Even books were published and purchased *before* the event, so all would remember. We owe these two undaunted women a great deal of thanks for bringing us all together that summer.

The Leininger families, at least 400 strong, gather every five years in the Lindenwood Park, Fargo, North Dakota. We have been attending these reunions for over 15 years. I find the affirmation and the affection to be an essential part of getting older.

Our cousin Hazel Leininger, whom I talked a little about in my first book, is the woman of courage who has the talent to get us all together and coordinate these events. Since she is now over 80, she feels she must retire from this activity, although she is still needed. Hazel had the will to gather family history and to bring our people together. We can’t thank Hazel enough for giving of her time and energy for so many years, just to keep the family united. She has these gifts of endurance, and of caring. Those Norwegian qualities are a real plus.

The Oetting families of our generation gathered together for small family reunions in the summer, plus weddings, funerals and special celebrations, but the older generations never organized large reunions like the Leiningers and Brauers.

Grandpa and Grandma Oetting spent over 50 years in Waterloo, Iowa, and were highly respected all over the state. He was admired in the ministry as well as in hospital administration. The boys and I would go to visit them, or they would visit us here. Mother Oetting was a grand, caring person and went out of her way to accept my new husband, Don.

She was not well, however. Soon after Walt died, she developed cancer. Pains starting in the hip were the first sign of problems. Eventually she was diagnosed with lung cancer. This dear woman died in the summer of 1969 at age seventy-one, shortly after their 40th wedding anniversary. She was buried near her son at Our Redeemer Cemetery here in St. Louis.

I was deeply saddened by her death. We had been close to her, and knew we would miss her great spirit. She had grieved for Walter, her first-born child. Maybe she also feared she would lose her three grandsons when I married Don.

There was not a particular move toward Don adopting the boys. We felt that all three would want to keep the Oetting name and heritage, so neither of us pushed for their adoption. Besides, when presenting Grandpa Oetting with the idea, he flatly rejected it.

My sons did use the Brauer name or hyphenated it with Oetting periodically. None of us liked the fact that the five of us did not have the same name, but there was not much we could do about it. We felt having the same name would bring us closer together. It is common these days to have different names, but not so twenty-five years ago. I still do not like having a different name from my sons. Now I on occasion use several of my names, like on the cover of my books!

In the fall of 1969, my good friend from St. Joseph, Michigan, the Reverend Martin Zschoche died suddenly of a massive heart attack at age 54. What shocking and sad news to hear about our long-time friend who used to write happy letters and even jokes to me after Walt died! We had been so close. I could not attend his funeral there in Frankenmuth, Michigan. It was too soon for me to bear another great loss. His memory will live on forever.

Scouting was the big activity in our household for years. All three of my sons took part. From the time they were eight, they became Cub Scouts. Tom led the way, the first to get his dark blue uniform and cap, with gold and blue neckerchief to match. That was one thing they followed each other in, one by one.This complete uniform was worn for den meetings, weekly pack meetings, and yearly Blue and Gold Banquets. At least one parent was required to attend the pack meetings and the banquet *at all cost*.

The Pine Wood Derby races were yearly, with a small racing car fashioned out of wood and entered in the race. It was both exciting and frustrating. My sons did not have a father who could help them make a car, as most boys did. I felt pretty helpless and sad at such times. Occasionally someone from church came over to give them some help, which was so nice. The pack meetings were the real endurance test for me. I was then a single parent and attended all these gatherings, which were noisy affairs to say the least! The 8-10 year olds were excited and enthusiastic about just getting together and sharing all they had been doing the past month. I still see the chaos vividly in my mind's eye! However, I look back on these memories with fondness.

Between Cub Scouts and Boy Scouts was Webelos, which was to prepare the boys for the big time, Boy Scouting. All three eventually went into Boy Scouts. They selected the merit badges they felt they could do. I helped them plan how to do them with the assistance of good merit badge counselors, and made myself available for them.

Working on merit badges was a way of life in our household for about ten years. Greg was the only one who attained his goal: Eagle and the *Pro Deo et Patria* Award. He received merit badges in everything from stamp collecting to caning chairs. He did an antique chair which he eventually inherited and now has in his home. Tom and Andy went as far as the "Life" award, then dropped out of Scouting when their interests changed. Now it was high school, girls, smoking, and friends for the older boys.

Gregory just seemed to keep his blinders on, keeping focused on his goals. I remember how it kept me on my toes just purchasing the merit badge books, driving him to each merit badge counselor, and making sure I was free and available when he needed me. Being a mother was definitely a full time job! Don and I even hiked with him in Forest Park and helped map out the number of miles required for the hiking merit badge. That was just one example of being there for this young man of ours who was forging ahead.

I always made myself available for all three sons. Opportunities were open for so many things, and I never wanted them to feel they couldn't do things because of my time or money restraints. I made no limits. I wanted them to have the freedom to do whatever they aspired to do, and urged them toward positive goals for their future. What seemed to happen along the way for the older boys was the influence of peers. In their search for an identity, they got mixed up with the wrong kids. So what does a teenager do when he hears by the grapevine that the world out there in distant lands (like California and Colorado) is bursting with excitement? The motto for youth and the counter culture was to *"tune in"* (music), *"turn on"* (to sex and drugs) and *"drop out"* (of society). Some wanted to "take over" the old and overthrow it -- whether it was old ideas, government, or the rich -- or do whatever "turned them on at the time." They followed who was leading at that moment.

In the early 1970s my two teenagers were drawn to this new world, and this new way of life, as many teens were. My eldest, Tom, dropped out of high school one afternoon, and took to the road. Hitchhiking was the mode of transportation, and stealing was the way to get food. There were communes across the country, places to get a good night's sleep and to share drugs.

In 1972 over 12% of high school students dropped out to partake of this new life, the highest rate ever (up to that point). Over twenty years later, we are slowly getting our kids to stay in school.

The shock of Tom's disappearance from school was a real blow to our family. From then on, it was a nightmare of desperation. Police were all but numb to the report of a missing teenager - so what was new? Thousands were dropping out across this land, and our cries for help went unheeded. What had we done to him, we asked ourselves. We had not abused our children. I believed in spankings applied at an appropriate time (and on the bottom) when they were young. So what was new? That was the way I was raised and I think I turned out fine. Guilt set in. It was vaguely mentioned among a few friends about others having "problems" with their teenagers. Nothing was talked about, because each of us felt we must have been *bad* parents to have such a fate befall our families. During those troubled times, Don had a very full schedule traveling a long distance to school, teaching music to young children, and spending many evenings and weekends involved in activities related to his profession. Many times I felt alone and overwhelmed in trying to solve the unsolvable. I have not told the details to many of our family members or friends. I used to be ashamed, and now it doesn't matter. Besides, I figure they may not understand, and they just might be critical of us. How therapeutic it would have been in those crucial times if we could have all freely shared our grief as we do today! But it was "shoveled under the rug" like all bad news in those days. You suffered in silence. I wonder how many parents are out there today still blaming themselves for their children's behavior. I hope they read these pages, just to let them know it wasn't their fault.

The police would let you know when they jailed your child for stealing food to survive, or just picked him up for one reason or another. Their big question was, would we pay for the bus ticket to ship one of them home... Of course we always did.

The arrival home of a delinquent son, accompanied by a police officer, was devastating for all of us. Here we had this child/man of ours at the door with nothing but the clothes on his back, with long disheveled hair, dirty clothing, and an embarrassed look on his face. We did not know what to do.

We knew after Tom's first taste of excitement "out there," told in glowing terms, that there was no hope for him staying home. He had made a conscious decision to do exactly what he was doing, and he was enjoying it. We were helpless to change his mind. How do you contain someone who is determined to do what he wants to do? One could not tie him to the bed post, as desperate parents did in some cases: the horror stories of bygone years.

For the most part, life was a busy nightmare those years between the 70's and 80's. Tom could sit for hours and tell his stories of adventure in this strange world of hippies and druggies to all of us. At one point, he hitched up with a guy named Barry, who was already in his twenties and well experienced on the road. The two of them decided our house would be a good stopover to hit for food. However, they made one miscalculation. They decided to *break* into our house, because we were gone. Bad decision! A neighbor notified the police, who caught them carrying out bags of meat from the deep freeze. To jail they went, but not for long. Out of empathy for their needs (or our temporary insanity), we gave them overnight lodging and lots of food. Barry knew how to pack it in. He explained his successful way of eating. The intent was to eat as much as possible, and eat slowly over a span of hours; that way it would last for a day or two if necessary (for instance, if no free food was available). Well, he ate and ate and ate. We did not know one human being could consume this much food over one long sitting! Tom was eager to be on his way, and this little interlude was strictly an inconvenience for him.

It was shortly after this day of eating and telling their stories of adventure that Andy took off from high school to get in on some of this fun. How could he go wrong? There was no responsibility involved. This must be a good way of life, he must have thought. Andy vanished for varying periods of time, as Tom continued to do.

By this time, I was in a state of disbelief and shock. How could I have two sons just roaming around the country? I was nearly paralyzed with fear and anguish about them, not knowing what to do or where to turn for help. Whom could I tell besides the police, who could not help either? Even then, a teenager had to be gone 48 hours before being listed as missing. This was a time when we really needed friends and their support. I decided to drop our usual Christmas Open House. What could we tell our friends? It was a sad time indeed!

As years rolled by, Andy returned for schooling at Bailey Technical School in St. Louis. He did not finish the one-year course, but did eventually get his G.E.D. (high school equivalency). Tom did too, later on. This was interspersed with some years of imprisonment for both boys, usually for stealing food in an attempt to survive on the road without money.

Once they were used to this transient life it seemed to be their chosen way. Without roots, being free, and without responsibility toward anyone, they appeared to live quite comfortably with themselves. There seemed to be no concern for family or their past ties.

Eventually Tom and Andy were both persuaded by judges to make the decision to mend their ways. Their other choice would be eventual permanent residency in prison. Gradually this free way of life gave way to some responsibility for their own behaviors.

Andy first joined the Navy, knowing that he needed strong guidelines and parameters to get him back to a responsible way of life. It was a rough road, but he was proud when he completed an Electrician course while in the service. We were very happy for him. The Navy had no use for guys smoking marijuana, however. It was rough to remain drug free, and Andy again found himself out on the road.

Tom finally landed a job in St. Louis, but jobs just did not work out for long. That was the major problem for both Tom and Andy. They had been around their peer group for so long, using drugs, and practicing no responsibility, that getting to a job and sticking with it was an insurmountable task. When things were not going their way, or did not please them, they left the job or were dismissed.

These two adopted sons, Tom and Andy, had a different genetic makeup, following a nomadic way of life like their biological parents. The environmental conditions of being fostered out as children, adopted, and then having their adoptive father die, were traumatic events affecting their self-esteem, self-worth, and sense of security.

To this day Andy is still trying to get his life in order, to make enough money for them to live on. It has been rough for him. However, he married a young woman in 1986 who has been his best support and friend. I'll call her Carla. She had lived around the Springfield, Missouri, area all her life. She, too, had many losses of family in her early years. Andy and Carla have this in common, plus they enjoy the same lifestyle of country living. Their life is simple, with few demands, which they like. Andy worked hard in getting his license for repairing small engines, taking a correspondence course through the mail. He graduated and is proud that he completed this course of study. Carla is equally as pleased and so are we.

Andy's brother, Tom, who had the same biological parents and thus the same genetic composition as Andy, has had an equal struggle to find his niche in life. Finding something he could do which he liked, and could make enough money to live has been a struggle.

Over these many years, Tom would give us an occasional call, just to let us know he was still alive and kicking. However, there was a span of seven years where he did not make contact with anyone in the family. We were sure he had met his fate somewhere on some foreign shore. I was quite concerned. After all, I was his mother, at least the only one he knew. We had had a few good years and he was family, even though he had more or less rejected all of us long ago. He said he just did not want to have any ties or owe anything emotionally to any of us. One day in late summer of 1991 he called. No excuses, he just needed to talk. I was quite shocked and hurt that he had not cared enough to call or write all those years. He was surprised that it had only been seven years, he said. I vacillated between anger and disappointment. We talked and cried for an hour.

Tom did have a reason to call, however. He needed to tell me he and the young woman he was living with had a baby boy, also named Tom.

Their baby, now at nine months of age, was in desperate need of a liver transplant. How terribly sad! How powerless I felt. What could I do? The baby was running out of time, and was on a long waiting list for a transplant. Tom knew his own child was in deep trouble. That was the way Tom was - he would call only when *he needed to talk*. I believe he never thought about my feelings, or if I just might be worried about him when he did not call.

With this phone call, I now had the opportunity to tell him about the deaths of his grandparents. Tom also was the recipient of a fair amount of money from Grandpa Oetting's estate. Grandpa had discussed this with me some years back. I felt it important to avoid dissension among family members at all cost. "Could you remember all three of my sons?" I asked, although there had not been any communication from Tom and Andy in their adult years to their grandparents or any relatives (or to each other, for that matter). What was legal was right. All three of my boys were legally Oettings. Grandpa Oetting remembered all three in his will. Justice was served.

Around Christmas time of 1991 we tried to reach Tom again by mail, but there was no response. Then we had a telephone conversation with a friend who was staying at his place, who told us Tom's baby had just died in the hospital somewhere in California. He knew nothing more. We have not heard a word from Tom since, and he has not responded to any cards or letters. He has once again faded off the face of this earth... Only God can take care of him now.

When the boys were young all three had worked at Camp Pioneer in New York for short periods of time during the summer months. Although they were not of age, they would work in the kitchen or with the grounds crew. Gregory at age 12 was tall, over 5'4" and 111 pounds, and he proved himself to be responsible and strong. He had the job of "Pop Boy," which he did diligently and with great pride, filling the pop machines throughout the day. Between 12 and 13 years of age he grew 7" and gained 24 pounds! It must have been all that coke and hard work! His pay was small, but he had the greatest experience for his future. He had a big responsibility at an early age, and could handle it. He took pride in doing a job and doing it well. This was the most important lesson he could learn. Another important facet of his learning to deal with people, was convincing the "powers that be" that he *could* do this job. They *trusted* his judgment and *gave* him *a chance*. It is hard to believe he was only 12. That was 1973, the last summer we were at camp.

After we were married, Don had come with us and was the Program Director for two summers, but the irresponsible behavior of the teenagers at camp was getting to him. He wanted his summer off. Greg and I went just that last summer alone. I needed to be home during the summers that followed, because of the erratic behavior of Tom and Andy.

The wildest I ever got during this "Age of Aquarius," was wearing my dresses just slightly above the knees (no miniskirts for me). Teasing hair followed by plenty of spray was done by most of our generation. No wonder our ozone layer weakened! I still have my expensive purse with the leather strands hanging from it.

Don and I sang and danced our way through these summer camp years with satires on "Society" and "We're a Couple of Swells." Several of us women did a pantomime from Rodgers and Hammerstein's South Pacific, "I'm Gonna Wash That Man Right Out Of My Hair." These performances each week made roughing it tolerable. Music, square dancing, sports, and devotions around the campfire made for a pleasant summer reprieve.

There was special time for crafts during camp hours. Greg was particularly fond of getting into all the projects with gusto. He liked doing things with his hands: whether it was drawing, painting, ceramics, or vinyl and leather "boondoggling," he did it all. He was quick and he was eager. He made gifts for everyone. All the relatives were recipients of those ceramic ashtrays (if they smoked), or a nice leather chain with a pendant or cross hanging from it. These were very popular and you just weren't in fashion for camp if you were not wearing some "boondoggling" around your neck. Many designed and painted their own pendant from a piece of shale or other natural material found on the beach.

Since those camp days, I have not truly enjoyed summer. We had a plan for seven years and it worked. The withdrawal of that summer relaxation was difficult for me, but my priority was always to be there for my family.

Greg and I continued the leather work at home; we even put up a booth to sell our wares during an annual money-making affair to support Jefferson Grade School in Pasadena Hills, where he attended. Greg loved

Christmas and was eager to give gifts, buying little things for the family at these fund raisers. In no time he would have them wrapped and ready to give away at Christmas!

Gregory was my eager helper in stuffing and stamping Christmas cards and letters too. Around 200 was and still is the average number I send. A yeoman's job, but I figure this is *one* time in a year so many of us communicate. We seldom saw our "old" friends and relatives.

I look back with pride on those days when Greg was a boy. It just warms my heart so much. His kindness and generosity were unusual. I never cease to wonder how he maintained his positive attitude, forging ahead no matter the negative things that daily surrounded him. I realize he came by some of it genetically, but he was especially blessed as well. I need not wonder how he could get through a six-year residency in neurosurgery!

During these very trying years for the family, Gregory maintained his drive to learn in school as well. He needed to study, and his ability to concentrate was good. It did not come easily as with some children. He worked for whatever he received, and never slacked off or gave up. As a high school student, he was a straight A Honor Roll student who took pride in his accomplishments. Of course we did, too.

He played tennis and soccer, but the violin had to be shelved as there was not an orchestra at Lutheran High School North. We felt sad about that, but then his interests were expanding. Young women came into his life, and he got along well with them. Don and I also maintained our encouragement, and worked at not taking him for granted. Do not forget, we had two sons who had dropped out of high school. We did not know if our third child would do the same... What was our guarantee? I did not let fear overwhelm me, but it was there, lurking, wanting to envelop me. When one talks about praying without ceasing, well, that is what I did. Only I also pleaded and demanded that God please guide Greg's every moment, and ours. I trusted that He would not fail us because we *believed* that He truly is a loving and caring God. It is not God's fault that man makes mistakes or fails. It is man's failures.

During those hectic years as our neighborhood was rapidly becoming integrated, I was appointed by our Mayor Meckfessel to serve on a newly formed Community Relations Commission for our City of Northwoods. About 12 of us were brought together to assist in merging our two cultures, Afro-American and European American, into a peaceful coexistence.

This commission was made up of whites and blacks who were supposedly open-minded and believed in peaceful coexistence. In other words, the whites weren't planning to run, and the blacks weren't too hostile toward whites to talk. None of us were basically shy. We maintained a free and open communication and got along well. In essence, if our group could be a model for our city the rest of the neighborhood would follow. That is basically what we did. We kept a watchful eye on what was happening in the community, wrote reports to the Board of Aldermen, made suggestions for improvements, and provided for a peaceful reorganization of our Four Wards Civic Association. Both blacks and whites were elected as officers in each ward. We received good local publicity through our Northwoodsman newspaper, and had opportunities to tell about the work of our Commission in a crowded Town Hall Meeting, which we planned and executed.

The Aldermanic Board felt a bit intimidated by our group at times, but we did not worry. We had been appointed by the Mayor. With the reorganized Civic Associations, everyone felt they had an *equal* opportunity to serve; this was a major step and a very important one. It took *time* and *effort* on everyone's part. Nothing came easily. The whites who were disgruntled left. That was good as it made our job easier. We kept a watchful eye that the ordinances were being followed and housing stock maintained. Our Aldermen were kept very busy.

During this time, I was contacted by St. Louis University's Institute for Peace and Justice, under the Visiting Professor, Dr. Anima Bose, from India. She asked me if our Community Relations group would have a panel discussion on our work for equality in our city. It would be open to the students and the public. We felt honored, and eager to share our learning experiences.

November of 1971 we had a roomful of folks willing to learn. How thrilling and exciting! The topic was "How to Develop Human Relations Through Mutual Understanding and Living Together in a Community." It went over very well.

I developed some very close friendships along this path to peace. Some of our group, myself included, became a part of the Committee to elect the first Afro-American person ever to the Normandy School Board, Florence Hill. She was a resident of our city of Northwoods, who had a highly qualified background in education, with a Master's degree; as well as being an experienced and caring person. Florence had the qualities of good communication skills, without fear of expressing her opinions and feelings. It was an exciting time and I felt revitalized being a part of change, and opening up opportunities for blacks. We could make a difference. That was a good feeling. We were making history in our little community of Northwoods, and we loved it. At least I felt I was doing something that just might help bring peace and a better feeling between blacks and whites (even though we had little peace of mind at home).

We passed out literature *carefully* during this history-making election. There were still many hostile white folks in our midst in the School District. We did not wish to add fuel to the fires of hatred. We knew who some of those folks were, and stayed away from them if possible. Generally, we felt there was acceptance of this new idea of putting a black person on the school board. However, it was not proven to us until after the election. *We* won! *She* won! *Florence Hill* was the *first* Afro-American person ever to be elected to the Normandy School Board. How exciting! I distinctly remember how happy and relieved I was! At last, I could *be* and *feel* a real part of bringing people together. This was 1972.

I was tempted to run for Alderwoman in our 1st ward many times, but felt I had three strikes against me: first of all I was a *woman* (we still have only one woman on the board), second a *white woman* (whites are in the minority), and third, a *protestant white woman* (in a largely Roman Catholic community) and one who didn't like rejection! Besides I was very busy with my family and other activities so I never did run for a political office.

Other activities I participated in were volunteer nursing at our Lutheran Medical Missions Clinic in Kinloch, a poor black community. This was a challenge I enjoyed. I felt a part of a team of doctors and nurses who cared for *all people*. My own doctor, Dr. Harvey Liebhaber, was a part of that team, bringing future doctors from Washington University School of Medicine to assist.

I also volunteered my services twice a week, working with the counselor at Jefferson School where Greg attended grade school. I filled in for her alone after she had a baby. The sixth graders gathered in small group sessions to talk about feelings. Black and white children shared eagerly. What an opportunity to learn respect for each other at an early age! I was thrilled and hopeful that we would always have peaceful coexistence.

I joined the Board for Lutheran Human Relations in St. Louis around that same period. We were another enthusiastic group of blacks and whites, who coordinated get-togethers with our Missouri area churches and agencies. I became the resource person, researching books and materials, purchasing them for displays, and selling them at these gatherings. We were the resource for many folks wanting to know about integration. We told them it would work, if we took the time to *care*. It was God's will that we live in peace in our world with *all* people.

Our group in St. Louis was always well represented at the national gatherings of human relations people at Valparaiso University in Indiana. This large group was coordinated by great folks like Karl Lutze assisted by his faithful wife Esther. This national organization still exists today; however, the St. Louis group discontinued activities as local agencies carried on the task. Lutheran Family and Children's Services is one of those that provides services for counseling, food, and clothing for the poor and needy. Men like LeRoy Zimmerman and Otis Woodard were hired by this agency in those early years to facilitate this work. They continue to serve the needy in the St. Louis area, as well as the thousands of flood victims in 1993.

Otis was ordained our Minister of Reconciliation for Lutheran Human Relations in those days. Otis made himself accessible to the needs of the poor, and developed a distribution center for food and clothing. This center, which is very active today, is also where he lives. Otis is one of these tremendously happy and generous folks who would give you the clothes off his back. I do not recall ever seeing him without a smile. I would literally bump into him many places, and be gathered into a great bear hug in a flash - he was so happy to see me, and I him. Otis is especially blessed with the gift of healing emotional wounds, and bringing many diverse people together. He had the ability to be open and honest about whatever he said.

I was on the Lutheran Family and Children's Services Board from 1977-83 so you know I had many hugs in those days! I needed them desperately. Otis always made me feel like one of God's special gifts, just as he was. Life was a continuous celebration for him, which he showed in his selection of clothing. His wife made his shirts of many colors like Joseph in the Bible. Hanging from his neck were a minimum of six strands of beads, chains, or baubles representing someone or something. He never let on that he too was suffering. His eager laughter never betrayed the hurt inside. They say that anyone who can laugh a lot has suffered a lot and that laughter is a sign of suffering. How true. Otis reminds me of an Indian Chief: representing his race and God's love.

Otis speaks in churches, schools and civic groups all over the state of Missouri, playing his ukelele and singing about his love for Jesus. He received national attention when he was in a public film on social issues.

Everyone knows Otis, rather *everyone* who cares about people and their needs. I recently talked with Otis on the phone as I had not bumped into him for a while. He now has *nine* sons, and they all have the name of Otis. You have it right, *Otis*. However, he tells me, with a laugh, they have other names, and assured me he does have three girls and they aren't *Otis*!

He is no longer employed by Lutheran Family and Children's Services, he says, but he now owns Lutheran Outreach North, and it is going strong. "Currently I'm providing housing for young pregnant teenagers until their babies are born. I have five places to house unwed teenagers. Hundreds of schools across this country, even Canada and Mexico, invited me to talk to huge audiences about safe sex or no sex. Kids are sexually active today," he muses, and is amazed at how young. "Two pregnant *eleven* year olds were in one of my homes recently."

He is truly carrying out God's message to love one another. I feel inspired and hopeful for our world whenever I talk with Otis. He is one of God's most eloquent and genuine folks anyone will ever meet. He is a match for men like Jesse Jackson, who are undaunted in their quest for equality and justice.

The church at large was and still is struggling with these issues. We are about to discover in the years ahead just how painful the struggle can be.

Our Home

Gregory as he grows up

Greg, Eagle Scout, at 14

Greg's High School Graduation
June 1979

Our family in the 80's

Mom, Dad and Gregory during the 70's

Dad Oetting

Mother Oetting

Mom and Dad Leininger visiting us

Dad with my scouts

CHAPTER EIGHT

1970's Evolving
Our Parents' Health Deteriorating
Mother And Dad Brauer's Deaths

"He's Got the Whole World in His Hands..."

"Whatsoever You Shall Bind on Earth
Shall Be Bound in Heaven;
And Whatsoever You Shall Loose on Earth
Shall Be Loosed in Heaven."

Matthew 18:18

Don was continuing to go to work across the Mississippi River to Roxana, Illinois teaching young ones to love music. His hopes were and are that they would come to *appreciate* singing, and just maybe classical music. At least he was giving it his best try. In collaboration with the other music teacher, Corinne Podesva and Don wrote many of the musicals and Christmas programs which were presented a couple times each year.

The kids love to perform for their parents and friends, who turn out in large numbers, cameras in hand, to see and hear their children. As Don says, the older he gets the more he appreciates the variety of gifts God has given to all these growing little ones. They can be molded and influenced if we just take the time to *listen* to them. That brings to mind the song from South Pacific, "You've got to be carefully taught..." (It won the Pulitzer Prize.) The current thinking these days is that it takes a whole community to raise a child in these turbulent times. I believe that. All the families who are bringing children into this world must keep them close together, and give them the love, encouragement and supervision so essential.

My Don also had a variety of organs to play over the years, mostly pipe organs. He was the organist at the Chapel of the Cross in North County for about seven years. Interestingly enough, the choir director was the individual who was influential in selecting an electronic organ. We never quite understood how that all happened, when there was plenty of money for a nice size pipe organ. These political things do happen, we figured, but when Don was dismissed from his organ job "for playing the organ too loud," well, that was beyond our comprehension. What kind of politics was happening here? Could it be the same kind of political foray that was occurring in our church body at large? Don and I had been members of the Lutheran Church-Missouri Synod all our lives, both coming from a long line of Lutheran preachers, teachers and musicians who served the church well. Our Synod had been in turmoil for a number of years. The smoldering embers of dissent were fanned by a couple of newspapers printed by "men of the cloth." It was both shocking and frustrating. Mass confusion reigned in our church body. People in the parishes all over the country did not know who or what to believe. The fires had been started long before, between the "moderates" and "conservatives" in the church. When a *conservative* President of the Synod was elected in 1969, shortly after the election of a moderate

Seminary President, both based in St. Louis, we had the formula for controversy. Synodical president J.A.O. Preus considered his election a mandate to "clean out" the Seminary, which he did quite methodically in the succeeding years.

Some pastors, with or without their congregations, left the Synod. Many others, including most of our preacher relatives, stayed in our church body with the hope they could change things from within. The dropout was at random throughout the church at large. It was a personal, individual, and deeply emotional decision for Don and me to change church bodies. However, it was the most healing decision for us at the time. We joined the newly-formed Association of Evangelical Lutheran Churches (A.E.L.C), when Don accepted the organist position at Zion in Ferguson which was already a member. This church body merged with the American Lutheran Church (A.L.C.) and Lutheran Church in America (L.C.A.) to form the Evangelical Lutheran Church in America (E.L.C.A.) in 1988.

No "false teachings" were ever defined, but the St. Louis Seminary's Board of Control succeeded in suspending President John Tietjen, prompting the student body to declare a moratorium on attending classes until the issue would be settled. Most of the Faculty joined the student body in the moratorium. Weeks later 40 of the 45 professors were fired because of their protest.

February 19, 1974, all but about 70 students and five faculty ceremoniously left the campus forming the "Concordia Seminary in Exile." They continued their theological education wherever they could find classrooms; in particular, at a Jesuit institution, St. Louis University, and at the United Church of Christ's Eden Seminary. These brave institutions opened their doors to a courageous group of men and women. Nothing but God's love, their faith, and the strength He gave them, carried these Missouri Synod Lutheran students, professors and their families through the trials of the years that followed.

I will not go into great detail on what events happened before the "walk-out" occurred. There were a couple of books published by friends about the church's struggles over the years. The first was *No Room in the Brotherhood* by Dr. Frederick W. Danker in 1977, published by Clayton Publishing, Inc. in St. Louis. The former President of Concordia Seminary, Dr. John H. Tietjen, completed a detailed book about the conflict in 1990. It is called Memoirs in Exile: Confessional Hope and

Institutional Conflict, published by Fortress Press in Minneapolis. These books are well worth reading or scanning just to get a *feel* of the dissention in the church.

We were still reeling at this time from the effects of the sixties generation, Woodstock, race riots and burnings, the Vietnam War, draft resisters, flower children and the "Age of Aquarius." The pursuit of peace in marijuana, LSD and alcohol abuse came to a dead end for many, literally. The search for a "Utopia" was winding down. "If it feels good do it" was not the answer. When four Kent State University students were shot by the police during demonstrations, the era was over.

Some "activists" were living in communes all over the countryside, while others carried on their quest to rid society of what they considered a problem, the large institutions. Some went underground as the "Weathermen," attempting to bomb large buildings.

The "Black Panthers," formed with a less violent thrust, beginning the "Black is Beautiful" slogan to build self-esteem, as well as emphasize the positive attributes of being Afro-American. Large "afro" haircuts and dashikis were worn. The "Black Power" symbol and fist salute with Stokely Carmichael and Malcolm X originated out of this group of activists. Many young black Americans chose African names and some emulate today what these men espoused. Great men like Justice Thurgood Marshall must be given the credit for changing our system from within. His support of black lawyers, mayors, and politicians has made the *real* difference in shifting some power toward Afro-Americans. His death in the spring of 1993 saddened many people and cultures.

In the 1920's, the women marched to have the right to vote, yet today we are still struggling for equal pay. The fact that women still receive 59 cents for every dollar paid to men is emphasized today. So many of our women are single parents, divorced, and poorer than ever in body and spirit. The "Women's Liberation Movement" demanded equality. Some rid their bodies of bras, girdles, bouffant hair-dos, makeup, and anything that they felt bound them to the controls of the past. Women like Betty Friedan, author of The Feminine Mystique, Congresswoman Bella Abzug, and Gloria Steinem were the big leaders who pushed for equality for us. Gloria Steinem is still working today on the issues of equal pay for equal work, better jobs and conditions in the work place.

The "Gay Liberation Front" came out of the closet in full force, the largest group being in San Francisco. American Indians were some of the last minorities to get their feelings of oppression out in the open. Other groups are slowly evolving, as they feel the need for empowerment, and wanting to take control of their own lives.

More issues and marches are before our eyes on national television every day. Pope John XXIII said "How strongly does the turmoil of individual peoples contrast with the perfect order of the universe." After Vietnam, Nixon and Watergate, there was little hope for a better world. Trust in our government was virtually gone.

Many hippies moved back to the cities, finished college, and went on to a "regular job" in the very system they had fought against. Even today, many of these people still feel that just living together outside of marriage is a suitable way of life. Our divorce rate has gradually doubled. What was been happening to the children? We are now seeing how many of those children are suffering from the life style of the 1960's. Some are carrying on the attitude of their parents, that anything and everything goes, and "letting it all hang out." Venereal diseases and AIDS are now killing many. What happened in the 60's and 70's is affecting us so poignantly today.

The "Great Society" of Lyndon B. Johnson was to provide education, housing, and empowerment for all, including the poor and minorities. He wished to eradicate racism and poverty, but that did not work. We were scarred and skeptical. He was responsible for the Voting Rights Act of 1965, 100 years after slavery, removing many barriers that did not allow blacks to register to vote.

Even the astronauts proclaimed there was a great Creator who made this beautiful planet; but there was little true joy in the hearts of many. When the 144 hostages returned from Iran we again felt uplifted. Maybe there was hope for our country. Our troops in Vietnam were coming home in 1972 hopeful it would be the last devastating war. At the end of 1972 Hanoi agreed to a cease fire, and we sat down at the peace table. January 27, 1973 the Peace Treaty was finally signed.

The Vietnam War lasted two decades resulting in the deaths of five hundred thousand Americans and millions of Vietnamese, the worst devastation and loss of American lives since the Civil War! So many of the troops returned home broken physically and emotionally, their homeland split on the justification of such a war. The Anti-War movement began to fade when so many maimed and dead soldiers came home to our institutions and cemeteries. The veterans came home, but were forgotten. We did not want to be reminded of this tragic war. Now over 20 years later most are willing to admit it was wrong; however, many lives remain torn apart from the injuries, from flashbacks of the war, and from abuse of drugs and alcohol.

Death was a relief for many young adults in their prime of life. Others were institutionalized, not knowing who they were or why they existed. My heart goes out to the hundreds of young people who experienced an early demise, and to their families my deepest sympathy and understanding. Unfortunately, the institutionalized church is not able to convince many that God is the answer for confused lives.

The whole movement of the sixties and early seventies alienated many. Some got tired of it, and more forgot what it was all about or how they had reached such a disastrous end. Their idealism was ruined by their errors, and their enthusiasm faded by an unclear cause.

How quickly, it seemed, those years went by... In my mind's eye I see it all: a muddle of chaos. Not a pleasant memory. However, we do not want to totally forget it for fear it could be repeated.

Are there any lessons learned from that decade? It is hard to say. More open communication has been a by-product of those years. People found that drugs did not ensure happiness and peace. Depression, confusion and refusal to take responsibility for one's behavior ended disastrously.

We were nearing the end of the "Hippie Era" when I began working as a part time clinic nurse on the campus of Washington University. I later accepted the position as their night nurse in the Infirmary. We were still seeing the last of the "hippie types," as I will call them, with their accompanying problems; some with hair lice, fleas, abuse of drugs, depression and guilt from too much living and not enough studying. The pressures to be gay or not to be gay were all part of this era.

Juxtaposed with my Infirmary job, was another position I could not turn down. I was asked to be on the Faculty Panel for the St. Louis University School of Medicine, Community Medicine Division. As a nurse coming from the Normandy area, I would have a half dozen medical students assigned to me. I worked with the students as a resource person, with Nick Fjone as coordinator of their health projects.

The students would select health issues, matching their educational interests with our needs in the community. One of the most pressing health problems in our area was elevated blood pressure in young black males. The Normandy Senior High was selected for a special project to document information on this subject. It was of utmost importance to the Department of Community Medicine.

Prevention of disease and promotion of health was the goal of Community Medicine. Much controversy has evolved historically around prevention vs. cure. Prevention was dull for a new student. Cure, which involved working on cases in the hospital setting, was interesting and exciting. This controversy is still present today. The term doctor literally means "teacher." Improving the health of patients through education could save lives. However, the *individual* case with an illness is more controllable, lucrative, and satisfying to treat. Young medical students knew that a physician's foremost loyalty is to the patient as a person, as clarified in the Hippocratic Oath. It was a real challenge to get them excited about early prevention of problems.

These same groups of medical students began Health Fairs under our guidance. Nick Fjone and I were the coordinators of several Health Fairs, giving us first hand experience in prevention. The goal was prevention of disease through learning how to care for oneself. This was the driving force that led me into school nursing. My feeling was that I could have some influence on the young people in learning to care for their bodies. I was able and eager to teach them; getting their attention was the challenge!

St. Louis University did the right thing in making the decision to stay in a decaying area (in the 80's) and work for justice and change. They give their medical students the supreme education of hands-on experience dealing with people in the whole community. Father Reinert led the university firmly and with courage through most of the 20th century, first as the President and then as Chancellor of St. Louis University. Thank God for people of vision like him. He knew God would see them through the rough waters to victory.

St. Louis University stands today as an ever brighter beacon in the Grand Center area. Their message of hope for social justice burns clearly as a model for all our communities. This is the university where my Gregory proudly received his medical school education. More talk about that in a later chapter.

Our parents' health was slowly deteriorating during those years. My mother had a heart attack in 1974, leaving her with another bout of depression, less severe than the last, but a persistent problem. She never really recovered, but medications kept her functioning. Her eyes betrayed that profound melancholy which her heart held from childhood. The losses which I talked about in my earlier book, My North Dakota Prairie Childhood, remained vivid in her memory.

In his old age, my Dad stood tall, slim, and straight, as in his youth. He had a will of iron, and the courage of his convictions to match. He was a golfer and No. 1 bowler even in his eighties. Dad served the Lord as a preacher for nearly sixty years. As his mind pressed toward old age, the oxygen was not reaching the brain adequately. His judgment became impaired, followed by "near misses" in his driving. The car showed telltale signs of these little accidents, but the angels were riding with him! Mom did the "driving" and Dad was behind the wheel with his foot on the gas pedal, a dangerous combo! They managed to get around during his semi-retired years, even assisting Pastor Braun at Bethlehem Lutheran Church in St. Paul, Minnesota.

"You do what you have to do," particularly in old age, they say. However, Mom's nerves were getting frazzled. She was worn out from her "back seat" driving all those years. We figured they would surely end up dead on the highway. Not true.

After Mom could not "handle" Dad and his driving anymore, they moved in with us in St. Louis the fall of 1981. Her nerves were shot. Dad absolutely should not drive anymore was the word out. It was a simple problem to resolve. Dad and I made a deal. He would give up driving if I could get $1500.00 for his old Pontiac LeMans, and he would be satisfied. No problem - one ad and it was a done deal! That was the end of sixty plus years of driving. He never questioned his decision - no comment ever again about driving! "The Lord does work in mysterious ways, His wonders to perform!" More about my folks later.

Don's mother, Wanda, years ago had been striken with cancer of the bone (originating in the parathyroid glands) just when he left for River Forest College in Chicago. Brother Roland had been drafted into the Army around the same time. These factors, the family speculated, may have brought on the cancer. This strong woman from the little town of Kramer, North Dakota, no longer had her five sons to feed, to love and to care for. No one enjoyed her children more than she. Her pride was in her handsome, fun-loving sons, and now they were gone! What was she to do? She had been raised on the farm and knew no bounds as to what she could or would do. We Leiningers knew the Brauers as children, and had a great respect for what Wanda was about. She managed those five active sons well, and she felt there was no woman worthy to marry one of them! They all found wives quite worthy anyway. None of us was a match for her powerful personality, but I could hold my own. All five of us women have held onto our men.

Wanda cared for her "Shatz," Fred, with boundless energy, even later when she was on crutches. She had an endless series of radiation treatments over the 25 years she lived with that dreadful disease of cancer. It was unreal how she could keep going.

They retired to St. Louis and bought a little home in Florissant about the time Don and I were married. Don's Dad was 14 years his Mom's senior. He was experiencing minor strokes, and later he too developed cancer. Mother Brauer had her hands full.

Her cancer had reoccurred in the hips around 1974. I took her to Barnes Hospital for her last radiation and chemotherapy treatments. To this day, I vividly remember the look of amazement on the doctor's face when she came hobbling into his office on crutches, showing him she was still on her feet! He actually said he could not believe she was still around! That remark we felt was insensitive. It angered and frustrated both of us. I had all I could do to fight back the tears. That doctor did not know the endurance of this woman, needless to say!

Don and I and his brother Paul and wife Lois managed to care for his folks' needs over a number of years, while they still managed to live in their comfortable home on Wycomb Street in Florissant. Their car, a Chevrolet Bel-Air, was their means of transportation, but it was becoming a hazard for them. Dad Brauer's final drive behind the wheel came when he drove *down* an *up* ramp! I had been following close behind, as he needed repairs on his car. I remained at the top of the ramp honking my horn and watching in horror. I could not stop him. He realized his mistake as he slowly traveled down the ramp, turned around at the bottom and returned up that same ramp! The angels were also riding with him. This man of God who had served the Lord 60 years was especially blessed. He would not meet his death in a car accident either.

We drove straight home that morning. I relayed the tale of horror to Mother Brauer. With emphatic phrases and a long speech, she declared a moratorium on his driving. He may have been happy it was all over, who knows. The effort at age 83 was too much anyway. With those sad eyes he agreed with his "Schatze" as he endearingly called his Wanda. (It means someone very precious.) The car was sold, and it was never mentioned again.

After that Mom Brauer increased her baking, which she loved to do, just to reward the many folks who helped take them to church. They were members of Salem Lutheran Church in Black Jack at the time. The four of us "kids" (Lois and Paul, Don and I) did the many errands, helping take care of the house and yard, and generally caring for their welfare. Our kids pitched in whenever we needed extra hands.

In 1975 came the sad day when Mom Brauer finally realized she could not care for her "Schatz" any longer. She wanted to do it, but just could not take care of him and herself too. She put him in the nursing home at the Lutheran Altenheim one summer when we were on vacation. Her job was done on this earth. She had taken care of her Shatz and she had no other reason to keep going. Wanda had taken good care of him for over 50 years, and now it was time to call it quits. She decided when it would be over. One Sunday a month later, she called us, crying from pain and sadness. She could not stay in that house any longer. Mother Brauer wanted to go to the Altenheim to be near her "Herzeblatt" (little heart), another name they called each other. Looking back, that was a very sad day for all of us - she had given up. There is no greater loss and sadness than to see the human spirit die. Her pain was too much for her to bear alone.

She went to the Altenheim at age seventy-one. A private room was made quite homelike, but she really did not want to be there. It was apparent that the fear of having so much pain, coupled with the reaction of the pain killers, had left her feeling totally out of control of her life. A neurosurgeon had been consulted months earlier about the severe pain. The decision was made to go ahead with a double cordotomy to deaden the nerve endings. We thought the risk of losing the ability to walk as well as control of the bladder was still worth being free from pain. It was a relief for her, and a relief for all of us. There is nothing that made me feel more powerless and sad than seeing her in severe pain. It brought back the horrifying memory of my late husband Walt's agony.

After the operation she could walk at first, but in a short time lost control of her body from the waist down. The wheelchair was her way to get around from then on.

She wanted to divide all her cherished possessions among her five sons herself, which she carefully did on days when we took her back to their home. We kept the house that year just so she could go back now and then. Such sad times these were!

Our families would get together on Sundays at the Altenheim and bring Mom and Dad Brauer together in their wheelchairs. The Altenheim staff was wonderful and tried to accommodate us at every turn.

She was there less than seven months when we were called to her side. Her vital signs were changing. Mother Brauer was dying. They had rolled her into a special room to give her nasal oxygen, and to keep a close watch over her. She still wanted to get out of bed. This powerful woman was not yet ready to die. Finally, she took her last breath on that day, November 9, 1976. She was seventy-two. Now she was in heaven. We could truly rejoice in the comfort that she was at peace with the Lord. In Isaiah 54:10 it says no matter who or what is taken away, the Lord's kindness and peace will always be with us. This is Don's confirmation verse and favorite passage in the Bible. (That was the year our country also celebrated its bicentennial, a year to remember.) Five days later her sister Lena also died of cancer. Dad Brauer seemed to understand that his Schatze had passed away, even though he rarely spoke anymore. He had hardening of the arteries like my Dad. He, too, quickly followed her in death four months later, on March 1, 1977. He was eighty-six.

Dad Brauer will always remain in my mind as the kindest, most patient and loving man I have ever met. I believe God prepared a special place in heaven just for him. They lie side by side at Our Redeemer Cemetery in St. Louis, just a few yards away from where Walt and Dad and Mom Oetting lie. Up the short hill is where our friend Bob

Duesenberg's parents are buried. Even my loving dog Coco is buried out there.

At the top of the hill is the memorial where Dr. Walter A. and Hulda Maier are buried. He was the internationally known Lutheran Hour speaker as I mentioned in an earlier chapter. His was a household name among Lutherans, a part of our childhood in North Dakota. His voice rang out over the radio every Sunday afternoon and we all listened. As we take walks around the cemetery checking monuments, so many familiar names appear before us, the faces now a passing shadow - some of Walt's old professors and their wives from Seminary days, friends and relatives, never to be forgotten. My Mom and Dad had cemetery lots there as well, but when Dad was old, he wanted to be buried near his family in North Dakota. His wishes were respected.

Our son Tom had met a nice young lady of Armenian descent in 1975. We liked his choice for a wife, but Marla's parents did not approve of their marriage. The kids were determined to get married regardless of family opinion. Neither of them had a secure job, but they felt their love could carry them. What could we say? We had no control over them; it was their life to live.

Don and I decided to help them out with the wedding plans; we gave them financial help and furnishings to get them started. It was quite an exciting time helping my first future daughter-in-law with her wedding plans. She even wanted to wear my first wedding dress! I loved that idea, and had it adjusted to fit her petite figure. We planned the wedding reception together and opened our home for the occasion. There would be a small group of friends and family attending.

Tom wanted to be married on his 21st birthday, so December 13, 1975 was the big day. Don was still the organist at the Chapel of the Cross then, choosing special music just for them. Our friend, Professor Ed Krentz, from Concordia Seminary, Pastoral Assistant to Pastor Nauss, had the ceremony. Tom had gone to Bethel School with the Krentz children, and liked the idea of Ed having the sermon. Gregory was the best man, a first time for him. He was already 6'2", 160 lbs., a slim fifteen year old teenager. Tom was of a slighter build, shorter, more wiry, and Andy was just a bit bigger and stronger built than Tom. The Navy would not give Andy leave on the big day, which was disappointing.

Tom and Marla's wedding was small, but lovely. It went without a hitch. We had hoped her parents would break down and attend, but no such luck. I felt sad for Marla especially, but she said nothing. That was the way they were, keeping all those feelings to themselves. Maybe their marriage would have worked out if these sentiments had been expressed. As it was, when they had anger or disappointment, they expressed it by running away from the situation instead of talking it out.

Within two years their marriage was all over. She started going out with another man, "keeping some variety in her life!" Tom was enraged, and could not be helped or consoled. I spent days with him listening to his anger, but nothing would comfort him. What a devastating thing to happen to this son of mine with a broken heart and spirit. None of us could believe this terrible thing. We shared his grief for the loss of this woman on whom he thought he could depend.

Tom reacted in a disastrous and desperate manner, ending up in jail on a work release program paying off bills after bouncing checks. What a time! What a tragic end of his hopeful future. There are no words to express our feelings of sadness and disappointment for him. He just did not seem to have a chance in life. Nothing seemed to work for him. His combination of genes and life's dreadful blows just was not in his favor. We were powerless to help him anymore, and he to help himself.

After paying off his debts, he decided the only thing to do was leave this area forever; which he did. I pleaded with him to stay near for family support, but he wanted to get far away from his bad memories. Tom liked adventure and went to Alaska and worked in logging camps for a few years, returning to a little cabin in the woods in the winter. He eventually purchased land there. Tom would call home on a rare occasion - usually when in distress.

On one of Tom's very bad times, he was beaten by several guys who wanted his recently earned money from deep sea fishing in the Aleutian Islands. His spleen was ruptured and had to be removed. Death was at his door he said, when he called me while recuperating. He made it through the surgery, but not without problems. The transfused blood gave him Hepatitis B which caused numerous infections. These troubled him for several years, he told me later.

Emotionally, all of these disappointments in the 70's affected the whole family. With the death of both of Don's parents, my folks' deteriorating health, Tom's divorce and eventual poor health, Andy's futile efforts to keep a job after being in the Navy, continuous efforts in fighting racism in our community, and leaving one church and church body and going to another; well, we were on an emotional roller coaster about ready to crash. We never knew what to expect from day to day. However, we knew that God was carrying us and He would never give us too much to handle as it says in the Bible.

I kept myself busy working at Washington University, the neighborhood, and physically and emotionally supporting Greg and Don. Don immersed himself in organ playing, and Greg in his studies, violin and scouting. Getting away from family difficulties helped keep our sanity, I believe. Greg was always there for Don and me, and we for him. He was as sure and steady as a wonderful spring rain, never wavering from the responsibilities he took on, though they were many.

He had followed his brothers at Shoney's Restaurant on Dunn Road, and worked there during his high school years. Greg had a drive to be busy all the time, possibly to avoid thinking about all the stresses at home and disappointment with his brothers. There was no way he wanted to follow in their footsteps. That was not in his genetic makeup.

During those busy high school years at Lutheran High North, just one mile from our home, he involved himself with several activities, one of which was acting. He was elated to get the lead part of Billy Bigelow in Rodgers and Hammerstein's "Carousel." This was his opportunity to sing and act, which he loved. We were so proud of him. (In the past, both Walt and I had enjoyed drama and had been in numerous play productions and Greg carried on this interest.) I had also joined the "Normandy Nomads" play group shortly after we moved into the Normandy area. A bunch of us "old gals" volunteered our time to do fairy tales across the St. Louis Metropolitan Area. We went to grade schools, day care centers, nursing homes and some hospitals, such as Shriners Hospital for Crippled Children. The pleasure was ours and theirs. I felt great joy and fulfillment seeing a room full of little ones laughing heartily. Even though it was an enormous amount of work and time, the camaraderie and shared pleasure kept me going. We did "Golden Goose," "Snow White," and "Sleeping Beauty," just to mention a few. They were written and directed by our talented Gini Bowie from the Normandy area. Some of the group are still doing plays under the name of the "Pasadena Players." Helen Beffa Preston faithfully and generously used her large home for readings, practice and parties. She was truly a talented woman who loved to share with others. We were deeply saddened by her death a few years ago. She will never be forgotten.

One day during these tough years, we received a shocking call from my brother-in-law, Reverend Louis Oetting, Walt's only brother. His wife, Sharon, age thirty-six, who was a registered nurse, was diagnosed as having a brain tumor. Louis described it as a growing web within her brain, although it probably was non-malignant, he said. The neurosurgeons were removing as much of the tumor as possible, with the hope that brain damage would be minimal. I need not say how much it saddened all of us to hear such news. This was 1976, a dozen years since Walt's death of a brain tumor, but it was like yesterday in my mind's eye. A flash of powerlessness seethed through me once again. How could she come through such a surgery and still be normal? My heart went out to Louis, Sharon, and their three lovely daughters, Marie, Angela, and Julie and their son, Jim. How could they manage if their mother did not pull through this formidable surgery? Many prayers truly went up to Heaven that day - God and the neurosurgeon's delicate hands were their only hope. The many prayers were answered in the months that followed.

She came through the surgery with some residual problems: damage to her "thermostat," some seizures, and the loss of her hair, due to radiation to rid the brain of growth in untouchable areas. Sharon has continued having increasing problems with seizures and has become disabled over these many years. Louis recently retired from the ministry to care for her. They moved in 1992 to the warm climate of San Antonio, Texas, near their daughter, Angela and family. He purchased a home with the amenities that will help in his continuous, dedicated care of Sharon. God has blessed Louis with an unusual amount of patience and love.

My sisters were a few hundred miles away in the early years, but in 1972 my sister Dorothy and her husband Wally Misterek left with their family of six children for Washington State. My sister Lois and her husband Bill Krenning followed with their three children the next year. Wally and Bill had been called to be pastors in the Olympia/Seattle area. We have seen little of my family since then, except on very special occasions like funerals or reunions. These pastors were fortunate to have moved out of the state of Missouri before the Synodical crisis of our church in 1974.

During these years of ups and downs between the 60's and 70's, we as a family pretty much kept our "troubles" to ourselves, fearful of others making judgment on our capability as good parents, or on us as people, as I said earlier. We kept the really troublesome problems under wraps; unlike the openness of today where many freely open up for scrutiny any aspect of their lives!

Greg's High School Graduation
June 1979

Elsa Zschoche Neusiis
with daughters Claire, Anita and Elaine

Greg - giving his Valedictory

Leaving home
What a sad time!

My Mom and Dad , 1970

Greg after graduation with
Grandpa Oetting
and God-father Duesenberg

Don, the proud owner
of a 1967 Austin Healey

Presenting scholarships
at LMC graduations

Many nursing teas

Rose Marie with Miss Kubler,
Instructor, Lori and Miriam

Mom having tea with Lori and me

Lori and I in full attire

Our 35th class reunion

School pin

As a school nurse

Reunions in North Dakota
with many friends and relatives

Sis Estelle and I

The Walter and Helen Leininger family

Cousins: Thelma, Alice and Bill, August Edith, Clara

Estelle, Mom, Ken Hazel and me

Ken and Hazel Leininger's family
John-Kay-Karen-Lynn
I was their "Hired girl."

Cousins: Bill and Nikki Rahlf surprised on their 25th anniversary

Leininger and Kensal reunion every 5 years

Doing the winter thing!

My Dad visiting his grandfather's grave, Boone, Iowa

Mom and I visiting her parents' grave Indianapolis, Indiana

Aunt Irene, Aunt Ida

Reunions in North Dakota with many friends and relatives ↑

One of Dad's churches in North Dakota: Bethlehem Congregation in the country

Mom with relatives, the Eickhoffs: Inez, Norman and Marlene, Olive

My involvement in children's plays

Celebrating Tanta Elsa's birthday with Lois Eberhardt and Alex and Betty Guebert

TRANSART Directors School 1980

Around the table again

Greg and I golfing while Don caddies

Committee to elect Florence Hill, the first Afro-American to our School Board

Patio visits

Bridge group: Bertrams, Lessmans and Breimeiers at our home

CHAPTER NINE

THE UPBEAT 1980'S
GREGORY'S GRADUATIONS: HIGH SCHOOL, COLLEGE, AND MEDICAL SCHOOL
HIS MARRIAGE TO AMY KUHN
DAD OETTING'S DEATH

"I live each day with hopes and prayers
for better days to be
And for the joys tomorrow holds
Beyond what I can see..."

Anon

"But the Fruit of the Spirit is love,
joy, peace, long suffering, gentleness,
goodness, faith, meekness, temperance:
Against such there is no Law."

Galatians 5:22-23

June 1979 was one of a series of proud and happy times for us at our house. Greg's continuous hard work and endurance had paid off. He was graduating from high school at Lutheran North with a GPA of 3.78, and a membership in the National Honor Society. We were delighted as a family when he was Valedictorian of his class! He had the honor of giving a speech at his graduation. The speech revealed many ideals of his that had come from me, and with tears flowing I listened to every word. I was so proud. Greg's self-esteem soared! I had also been saved from feeling I was a failure. Those stressful years of giving emotional support and being there for my Greg was paying off. Around 100 classmates, teachers and friends came for a reception in our home to honor this son who had proven himself worthy. He had risen above all the temptation to fall. What a time for rejoicing!

Our joy was mixed with sadness that following August when he was preparing to leave home for the first time. I was not ready for this son of mine to be hundreds of miles away. He had been accepted in pre-med at the University of South Florida, Tampa, a school which, Greg thought, would best prepare him for medical school. Besides, it was sunny and warm much of the year, and he was eager to get away from St. Louis' extremes of hot and cold temperatures. Well, what could this mother do but say nothing. I didn't want him to go so far away, and could hardly stand to see him leave. He had made up his mind, and knew what he wanted to do. I had always trusted his decisions, and did not interfere.

Loaded down with his material things and mixed feelings, Greg and I made the many miles to Tampa in his little yellow Fiat. This was his first car, his pride and joy. I helped him get settled into an apartment with another student.

With a very heavy heart, I returned to St. Louis via plane and to an "empty nest." How did those 18 years slip by so fast? We had been through all those tough years together, and we missed our family life together unspeakably. As a young person, he may not have realized the importance of his role and place at home. It was very rough emotionally for Don and me, as well as for Gregory.

I immersed myself in the new business I was starting as a Transart Designer. I called it "Les Beaux Art Designers." With a number of recruits working under me, we helped people select matting and frames for lithographs and etchings made by Transart Industries. I achieved a number of my goals, but I did not have my heart in selling. Several years later, I gradually phased out my business.

Greg soon tired of the miles separating us. After one year in Florida, he made the decision to move closer to home. He was so eager to get back to the Midwest he had the rented truck packed and was ready to return home by the time I flew there! I drove his non-airconditioned car by myself. There are few times that I can recall being utterly uncomfortable and worried at the same time! I did not know Greg's next plan for his future.

He was accepted at the University of Missouri-Columbia for the following semester, and finished his college education just a two-hour ride from home. It was nice for all of us to be together for some weekends. In 1984, he graduated *Magna Cum Laude,* and also became a proud key-carrying member of *Phi Beta Kappa*. We were bursting our buttons - our pride was overflowing! He was trekking up this difficult path to his goal with hardly a hitch. It was not easy, but he *was* going to be a doctor and that was it! Greg's stick-to-it-ive-ness, endurance and desire were always there.

We gave him a family brunch at a restaurant to celebrate this wonderful occasion with other relatives and friends attending. Gifts to help him on his way were a stethoscope, a sphygmomanometer, and two microscopes (one was an antique I purchased to help him remember the past).

This would be the last big graduation Grandpa Oetting would attend for Greg. He was so proud that one of his grandsons would be a doctor, a profession he truly admired himself. Grandpa was a charter member and Chairman of the Board of the Allen Memorial Hospital in Waterloo, Iowa, for many years. He had a deep interest in medicine and believed firmly in good patient care. His efforts toward this end were tireless. He openly talked about his own involvement spiritually and physically with patients, taking great pride in his work.

Dad Oetting had been living alone 20 years in their home after Mother's death in 1969. His life was very busy also as President of the Iowa East District of the Lutheran Church-Missouri Synod for many years. He served Immanuel Lutheran in Waterloo, Iowa, faithfully for over 50 years. Grandpa had been honored for his enduring achievements and years of service in the Ministry. These qualities endeared him to people all over Iowa.

Grandpa was healthy until the last three years of his life, when a sudden stroke left him weak and distraught. When a bout with cancer occurred and the ever increasing infirmities of aging hit, he required total care in a nursing home. The families gathered to celebrate his 90th birthday on April 25, 1989. He died 12 days later, and was laid to rest beside his wife, Edna. They are buried next to their son, Walt, at Our Redeemer Cemetery here in St. Louis. The Reverend Walter Dietrich Oetting was an institution, and to honor him they memorialized the hospital chapel in his name, a lasting memory of a man who gave immeasurably of his time and money for a needy cause.

As I continue to look back on the last 25 years, I wonder how we could handle the constant emotional turmoil with family and other factors out of our control that continually crept into our lives: I required a complete hysterectomy at the age of 39. Fortunately, the tumors were not cancerous. Our house was broken into around that same time, with little of great importance taken, but a big mess to clean up. A feeling of caution has pervaded my being since then. The theft of my two year old bronze Mustang, stolen right off the Symphony parking lot shortly after Don and I were married, was a shock and a big loss; but later having two cars rear ended by intoxicated drivers without insurance was intolerable to me! There was a limit. I spent hours filling out forms to have their driver's licenses removed just to vent my anger. After teenagers, I believe cars were our biggest problem, worry and expense. During that time, we had four cars of various ages and models. All were a "pain in *my* neck" to keep running! I assumed that major responsibility, because it was more important for my husband and sons to have transportation than for me to have a full time job when we were first married. I guess I did it, too, because I was the mother who stayed home most of the time and took care of things when they went wrong.

Don had a neat fire engine red Austin Healey, a 1967; the last year they made them, he says proudly. We frequently handed over $200.00 for minor repairs for it. Unreal! That was *a lot* of money in those days. Nobody in the family knew anything about cars, unfortunately. It was a fun car to own, but not to keep up. Our sons and all the many nephews thought it was the greatest experience riding in this little vehicle (with the top down, of course). We had that little sports car for a dozen years until money for medical school became the priority. I recall with a smile the day I picked up a total stranger from the airport who wanted to buy the car. He had seen our ad to sell the Healey in the Sports Magazine. This stranger came all the way from Atlanta, Georgia, in jeans, tennis shoes, and a *large roll* of *cash* in his pocket. He was buying the Healey to fix in mint condition, and sell (a deal already made) to a man in Switzerland. He was pleased with the car. Off to the bank we went where the deal was finalized. Don's car was driven back to Georgia and out of our lives forever. We later found out from this fellow that he had problems even driving the few miles out of Missouri! It had cost us enough, and I for one was glad it was gone. Don still talks sadly about his little sports car today. I believe he would buy another one tomorrow if he had the mechanical ability to keep it up.

Greg had caught that little sports car fever from Don, and we went halves on his bright yellow Fiat I mentioned earlier (dreaming that it would run like a top). That, too, was a major headache and he parted with it after the engine burned out on one of his long trips back from Florida. That sale helped a bit to pay for his college education. He has not forgotten that little fun car of his. I can just see him taking his kids out for a drive in his car of the future, a Lhamborgini (he says)!

Don did eventually get a big pipe organ to play in 1977, when Zion Lutheran in Ferguson asked him to be their organist. It did not take long after he arrived before an organ committee was formed. With both our Pastor Sam Roth's and Don's interest in good music, they pushed for a pipe organ. Martin Ott, a German organ builder, rebuilt and expanded an old pipe organ purchased from another church. This rebuilt Holtkamp is as fine an instrument as most organists appreciate playing today.

Each decade can be uniquely described by the dress and the music of that era. As we rolled into the *1980's* the style was still "leisure suits." Remember? That style with the loose casual jacket, and pantsuits made of the finest polyester were worn by everyone from the oldest to the youngest. Polyester was so easy to wash and most of all it required no ironing. What a boon for all of us who were tired of that tedious chore! No more baskets of sprinkled clothes waiting for some willing hand to stand for hours over the ironing board. Imagine how our Mothers felt! Even the men's dress shirts were polyester, but many preferred the cotton then and still do today. The younger set does not remember the "old days." They are out there buying up all-cotton garments. I still rarely succumb to an all cotton purchase (for fear it requires ironing). Only in a moment of weakness and a desire for high fashion do I give in. Fortunately, they are now making cotton that looks well without ironing!

Regarding the music, discotheques were out - heavy metal and hard rock bands were in for the younger set. Country and western made a strong comeback. For us it was still Bach, Beethoven, and Rachmaninoff, however.

The position of school nurse at Lutheran High North, just one mile from our house, opened up in the early eighties. I applied for the job and got it. Now I could continue with my goal of helping young people learn to care for themselves. I started band aiding every little problem at the school, and there were many. Some were interested in learning about being healthy and would come to me with their many questions. I recall one young man especially who stopped by on a regular basis (probably wanting to get out of class). He would sit and ask me numerous questions about specific diseases. He would keep the most astute nurse on her toes! I was highly motivated and managed to keep abreast of the fast pace of modern medicine.

In 1985, when AIDS was identified, I spent many hours reading Greg's literature and periodicals on what was happening in the world of medicine. Besides attending seminars at St. Louis University, I considered it a real challenge and a must to inform our students on the prevention of this dreaded disease of AIDS, and to promote their good physical and emotional health. As the fear of AIDS unfolded, and inadequate information was given over television, I wrote a lecture on this subject and presented it to the health classes. St. Louis University medical students also came to share a movie and answer questions on AIDS. Gradually the health teacher became interested in making this an integral part of the health class.

I had a health fair every year during those eight years as their school nurse. Although it was a lot of work, I had cooperation from teachers and students who were interested in prevention. I received a lot of personal satisfaction from this job as school nurse, but little monetary reward, considering my time, knowledge and intense interest. This situation seems to be eternal and universal for school nurses. Historically, a majority of school teachers and personnel seem to know little or care less about what a school nurse is about. I do not understand how this evolved over the years, or why school nurses are categorized with the secretaries and custodial staff. We are professionals who have spent years of study, and have hands-on experience in a hospital setting. Yet many school nurses tell me they are considered as "band aid queens" - they are something "less" since they are not working in a hospital setting. Our years of experience do not take priority. Without a bachelor's degree we count for nothing except hired help, I was informed. What a ridiculous notion, and an insult to our profession! Hopefully, attitudes have changed in the past several years I have been retired from nursing.

I am proud of the fact that I graduated from Lutheran Medical Center here in St. Louis and am a Registered Nurse. Loyalty to my school has been a big thing with me. Over these past 10 years in particular, I have been the Representative of the Alumni to the School of Nursing. I planned and coordinated ice cream socials and chili suppers for the students, and still present scholarships at cappings and graduations. These affairs helped us become acquainted with each other and with the Alumni. For many years I was on the committee to plan our annual dinner. Alumni members with spouses (if they have one) come from across United States, Canada and foreign countries. Some nurses married pastors from Concordia Seminary which explains our far-reaching membership. We still have an active alumni today.

My experience as a Parish Health Nurse in a low-income community was a very satisfying job. I had a grant from Lutheran Charities for this nursing job, which was helpful financially during part of Greg's Medical School. There is a great need for having a nurse available in parishes to assist the elderly as their health deteriorates. But there is only modest interest among pastors generally in having to *pay* a parish nurse. Thus many are volunteering their services, which is currently the expected norm. As far as I am concerned, we nurses are in the dark ages yet when it comes to being treated equally, (outside a hospital setting) and receiving the compensation we deserve.

We savored the joy and excitement of Greg's anticipated entrance into medical school in September of 1984. He had passed the MCAT exams in the upper 10% in the country. He had filled out many applications accompanied by the required fee, to numerous medical schools across this land already as a third year medical student. Next would come, hopefully, a request for an interview sometime during his fourth year.

In retrospect, and for the sake of all the doctors out there, these are the facts on what an *aspiring doctor* goes through long before entering medical school, from the parents of one (Greg graduated in 1988): Your life, from the courses you select to your behavior, is geared toward "how best to get into medical school." It begins in grade school and continues. You graduate from high school with at least a 3.8 GPA. You must be in the top 5% to 10% of your class and participate in extra-curricular activities. You go through four years of college, graduating again in the top 5% to 10% of your class with a GPA of somewhere over 3.8. While maintaining a "well-rounded student" status, the pressure is on to be as perfect as possible in every aspect of your life. You take the MCATS (medical entrance exam) for two days to see if you qualify for *an application* to medical school. If you don't come up to a specified rank, you are discouraged from applying. After this hurdle is passed, you write absolutely *perfect* applications and *letter-perfect* essays of why you want to become a doctor, accompanied with $50 to $100 per application (this was mid 80's). A minimum of six are sent all over the country. By now your desire to become a doctor is *internalized* to the degree that it is the *driving force* behind your very existence. If it is *not*, you will *not* make it into medical school, the plain fact is, you will *not* be accepted into a medical school, period.

If and when any of your applications are accepted, several medical schools may want to interview you - at a specified day and hour, all at *your* expense. Men and women already age 22-40 (many with a master's or doctorate in another field) are waiting with you to be interviewed. In your navy blue suit, white shirt and power tie or scarf (not flashy but with enough strength to show confidence) you are interviewed by administrative professors from the medical school. If at this point you might possibly be lacking in any area (which would seem remote) you can just forget being accepted - there will be no medical school for you. After a waiting period of six to nine months after the interviews you are then accepted into a medical school. *You are there*!

Our son was accepted into the St. Louis University School of Medicine in St. Louis, October 1983 for the fall of 1984. What a time for rejoicing! I vividly remember all three of us jumping for joy when Greg opened the letter from St. Louis University saying he had been accepted into the medical school! God had answered many prayers for all of us as a family. Getting into medical school is a *family project*, believe me! Greg had made it strictly on his own merit, besides constant prayer and encouragement. His depth of desire to become a physician was known truly only to the three of us, and at its greatest depth only to him. How I remember Greg's happiness! All three of us were ecstatic!

Now the realities of the cost of becoming a doctor were upon us. Greg had planned to get his education through the service, but his blood pressure interfered with that plan. Very little scholarship money is available for medical school, so we searched for every resource of available money to put up front for the first year: $13,500 for tuition, books, fees, equipment (which he had received as gifts), plus room and board. Total cost: over $20,000 for the first year. Each year we could expect a thousand dollar raise in his tuition, and additional costs for supplies, such as doctor's bag and all its necessary tools to give a good physical exam. By the last year ('87/88' school year) the tuition was $17,500. Costs were high but the desire and motivation were also high. I gave him a monthly income to take care of his physical needs as well as buying supplies. The loans paid for tuition, etc.

The hours were long: starting in third year he was "on call," and by fourth year he had "36 hour call," (the universally known test of will and strength) where you force your body and mind to do what would seem to be the impossible, done only by the will and the strength given by God, upon whom you solely depend. My Gregory was reminded of Mother's note (taped to the inside) every time he opened his black bag. It was from Isaiah 40:31 - "They that wait upon the Lord shall renew their strength. They shall mount up with wings like eagles; they shall run and not be weary; they shall walk and not faint." We just *knew* that God who is so loving, patient and compassionate would get him through even though proper rest and relaxation were not to be had.

Greg had an apartment mate after his second year in Medical School, Dan Satterwhite. They lived this grueling life of work and study together. This common bond of experience has sealed their friendship forever. God carried each of them and they in turn carried each other. When the times were really rough they both knew I would be there for them. Our method of communication was via telephone messages. They could count on me to rescue them from a mountain of dishes piled in the sink or mold on the bathroom walls!

Don did plenty to keep Greg afloat, physically and financially with his signature on many a loan for Greg. This whole process of getting through medical school, a joint family affair, was a venture I look back on with wonder and great satisfaction. How could Greg have done it alone? Without all the love poured out by his family, friends, his medical school counselors, and God he would not have made it. But to God all praise and glory!

Greg had another source of love and support to draw on; his friend Amy Kuhn. She had been a significant force in Gregory's life since early 1983. They had met on the University of Missouri-Columbia campus while in college that year. Both had a love for good music, and expressed it with singing. They had joined the "Just Singers" group affiliated with the University. Amy was two years behind Greg in school. He was bent on finishing his pre-med studies before getting seriously involved; however, they enjoyed each other's company. For the two-year period while Greg was attending school in St. Louis and Amy was still in Columbia they continued their relationship at long distance.

Amy graduated in the spring of 1984 and received her first teaching position in the St. Louis area, which was perfect for a continued relationship with a very busy medical student. She was very interested in the German language, stemming back to the days of her youth, when her father was an army doctor in Germany. Her interest continued through high school and college days, taking numerous courses for a future career in German and Math in preparation for teaching at the high school level.

Unknown to this young lady, she had also been preparing to become a doctor's wife throughout her childhood. Her father, Dr. Fred Kuhn, studied many years to become an Ear, Nose, and Throat Specialist. His father before him, Dr. Jack Kuhn, had delivered thousands of babies over fifty-some years as an Obstetrician. Most of the family's years after the service were spent in Oklahoma City where Fred's parents, Dr. Jack and Agnes lived.

Amy's Mom and Dad had divorced when she was around ten years old and are both remarried. Fred and Carol Kuhn and Charles and Bobette Keller are all wonderful people. She came from an expanding family, being the oldest of three children with a sister, Sherry, and a brother John. Like the generations before him, John is now in Medical School preparing to become a doctor. It is interesting to note the continuity of a family tradition.

In late summer of 1987 Gregory surprised Amy with an engagement ring. The time was right for both of them. He was entering his last year of Medical School, and she was beginning her second year of teaching in the Fort Zumwalt School District in the St. Louis Metropolitan Area.

Their engagement was a happy and exciting event for all of us. It was an especially important time for celebration and a time for dining. Every great event has been celebrated either around our dining room table or in the finest restaurant. It all depended upon how much time and energy I had. (This is probably true for most mothers.) Well, this was a very special happy time. We celebrated at a fine restaurant. None of Amy's family were able to join us because of the distance. Our good friends, Bob and Lori Duesenberg, and their children celebrated with us. Bob had been there for Greg when he was baptized, and always took his role as godfather seriously. He never failed over the many years to be a constant support for Greg.

And so it was that Gregory, my all enduring son, achieved his long awaited dream. May 19, 1988 came. It was the big weekend of his graduation from St. Louis University School of Medicine. There were two ceremonies, the first one at Powell Hall where honors were given. Gregory received departmental awards and honors in Biochemistry, Neuroscience and Research, followed by an induction into the *Alpha Omega Alpha* (AOA), the National Honors Medical Fraternity.

Two days later he was awarded the M.D. degree (Doctor of Medicine) at the St. Louis Arena when all the graduates from St. Louis University received their degrees conferred by President Lawrence Biondi, S.J.

At both of these ceremonies the parents were asked to rise and to pronounce a communal blessing on our children, to call down God's many graces on our graduating sons and daughters. With pride, Don and I stood and raised our right hand and repeated these words:

> MAY GOD OUR CREATOR BLESS AND PROTECT YOU.
>
> MAY YOU CONTINUE TO GROW IN WISDOM AND VIRTUE.
>
> MAY YOU USE YOUR KNOWLEDGE AND SKILLS FOR THE GOOD OF OTHERS.

MAY YOU BE STRONG LEADERS TO SHOW OTHERS THE TRUE WAY.

MAY YOU GENEROUSLY HELP ALL YOUR NEIGHBORS IN TIMES OF NEED.

MAY TRUE JOY AND HAPPINESS ALWAYS BE YOURS.

MAY LOVE AND PEACE ABUNDANTLY FILL YOUR HEART.

THIS IS OUR PRAYER TO OUR GOD. AMEN

At this point, the Doctor of Medicine Class of 140 men and women repeated the Hippocratic Oath. I was bursting with a pride and joy words can never express!

We did a lot of celebrating over this period of graduation days. Oetting families, Greg's fianceé Amy's family, and friends came to celebrate with us. Singing, dancing, eating, hugging and kissing were in order during those days and we did a lot of it! Greg's roommate, Dan Satterwhite, his mother Rose Mary and two sisters, Kirsten Duesenberg, who also had graduated from the university joined us with their families, of course. What terrific friends they all are! Our prayers of thanks and praise to our Heavenly Father were constantly in our hearts and minds.

St. Louis University with Father Lawrence Biondi as its President is carrying on the vision of Father Reinert, urging everyone, and particularly their students, to continue their service to *people in need*. The world is needing our helping hand to carry on Christ's message to "love one another as He loved us."

The culmination of many years for Greg of studying, working and planning were at an end. There is nothing that can express the joy our family felt that day. Gregory expressed his love, gratitude, and elation to Don and me with a gift of two dozen red roses delivered to our home. There was no need for words. We love him dearly and will do anything for him. Over 80 family members and friends came for an open house in our home to rejoice together. Amy's Mom, Bobette and her husband Chuck Keller stayed with us and immediately endeared themselves to us. Chuck, a dead ringer for a Brauer, stuck with Don and me making mountains of little sandwiches. His and Bobette's help was only exceeded by their enthusiasm for the occasion. What a joy it was getting more acquainted with Amy's fine family whom we had met a couple times under different circumstances. Even old and best friends of Greg's father, Reverend Walter and Herta Bauer, showed up at our door. How special that was! They wanted to see this young man who looked so much like his father, their friend Walt. Who this young man was who had inherited his brain power and stamina. (Gregory is willing to admit it came from *both* mother and father!)

Our spirits were dampened by the fact that Grandpa Oetting, one of Greg's biggest fans, could not be with us. He was recuperating from a bout with cancer and could not travel. Many gifts were opened and many memories shared that evening. Laughter and rejoicing rang throughout our home! We had not seen so much peace and joy on Greg's face before that day. He truly was a delight to behold.

Greg had been studying for Missouri State Medical exams during these last hectic months. A pass is required in order to *qualify for application* to a Residency program. He passed with high marks, while working 18 hour days as a 4th year medical student.

While looking ahead and making extensive preparations for his Residency, Greg was filling out applications, and also writing a "statement" on why he wanted to become a neurosurgeon. To be sent along with this information and each application, was another fee of $100.00 or more just to review it for the Neurosurgery Residency program. He sent a *dozen* out to various medical centers, mainly in the eastern part of the United States. Again for the residency program, he went through the same process of waiting to be invited for an interview, as he had done for medical school four years earlier. These days were challenging to say the least! After a half-dozen interviews across the country, Gregory was blessed with being accepted by his second choice, the Medical College of Virginia, Richmond (Medical Center). He was elated to be chosen by this Medical Center, surrounded by all the history of the South.

After Greg's graduation from medical school, he and Amy's plan was to be married on June 11. They had three weeks until the big day!

A lot of packing in Greg's and Amy's apartments began. To move and merge all of their material possessions to an apartment (already leased) in Richmond was a yeoman's job! Everything of his and hers had to fit into a 24-foot rented van. Everyone pitched in to help, and they were ready to leave within a week. Greg drove the van. Amy and her mother Bobette, sister Sherry, and brother John traveled the 15 hours to Richmond following the van in their loaded station wagon. Don and I stayed home to work, besides there wasn't any room to fit another person anywhere! We prayed unceasingly for their safe return in two days. Though tired, all returned to our home safely, having moved everything into Greg and Amy's future home. God blessed us all!

The next two weeks were devoted to preparing for The Big Wedding in Amy's hometown church, St. Stephen's Presbyterian in Oklahoma City. Much remained to be done before Greg and Amy tied the knot. Most of the plans were made by long distance calls, but all was going well. Greg and Amy stayed with us until leaving a few days before the wedding.

Don and I traveled to Oklahoma City, leaving here June 7, arriving at the door of Amy's grandparents, Dr. Jack and Agnes Kuhn, the next day. What a pleasure to meet such fine people. They opened their home to us in grand style. That same evening they invited their family and friends over to meet us. How nice! Their son, Amy's Dad Fred, had recently married a lovely lawyer, Carol, and they had a baby Carolyn a few months earlier. We realized we now have many more families to get to know and love.

The next day was occupied with fun things like the lovely bridesmaids' luncheon at the Greystone Restaurant. Don forgot to pick me up afterwards, so I was stranded there for a few hours chatting with the waitresses! The wedding rehearsal and dinner were that evening. Don and I hosted the rehearsal dinner served by the Sportsman's Country Club. We never did get to the rehearsal because the table arrangements had been changed from Any's and my original plan. By the time Don and I got the seating set the rehearsal was over. I was just a bit upset by this turn of events, but all else was well. We invited fifty-six family members and friends as our guests. All the families (of which we have many!) were represented: Oettings, Brauers, Kuhns, Kellers, Leiningers, Duesenbergs, and more. We shared many memories that evening. Tears flowed for the many happy times and the sad times. There was so much that so many *needed* to say. It was good. Sharing stories, along with hugs and kisses lasted three hours. We proudly call it one of the greatest therapy times we all have had!

And then came the big day, June 11, 1988. It was a lovely, sunny, peaceful day. We were prepared and waiting for Greg and Amy to become one. He was 27, she was 24. They had planned a long time for this major step in their lives. These two beautiful people understood each other, and accepted each other's faults. That was good. They loved each other - that was most important.

The hour was here. It was grand. The music so special - numerous violin solos by her uncle Dr. Robin Gunning, vocal solos by Amy's aunts, Sarah, Patsy, and Jaquelyn, a quartet by her sister Sherry and close friends, plus solos by Greg's Uncle Paul Brauer. Greg's Uncle Louis Oetting (his Dad's only brother) had the sermon and wedding ceremony. Amy's pastor, Reverend Ralph Ranney, officiated.

Amy's dress was gorgeous with pearls and sequins on satin and Chantilly lace. She was so beautiful with her long, dark brown hair fluffed just enough to fall softly around her face. Her six bridesmaids (including Maids and Matron of Honor) were her sister Sherry and close friends. They wore crisp, red taffeta tea-length dresses.

Gregory was so handsome in his black coat and tails! I was so happy for his happiness, and thankful to God for being so blessed. His groomsmen were his cousin, David Krenning, John Duesenberg, and other close friends, who wore black tuxedos. We mothers and fathers sat proudly in our finest clothes to celebrate this great event. We have wedding pictures all over our home reminding us of the joy of that day.

Greg and Amy's wedding reception was also at the Sportsman's Country Club where Amy's Dad held a membership. Good music was of utmost importance to them (as it had always been to our family) for the wedding and the reception. The sounds of a fine string ensemble greeted the guests as they arrived. After the buffet dinner, we danced the night away to tunes selected by another excellent group of musicians. Their honeymoon was one of their wedding gifts from Don and me, a week in Aruba, "the land made for honeymooners," they advertise.

After the honeymoon, Greg immediately began his first year at the Medical College of Virginia Medical Center in Richmond. The first year is called the internship year, a year spent at the hospital with "36 hour" call, sometimes three times a week. Now imagine the few hours he had with his wife, let alone anyone else. The fatigue experienced by these men and women is something that you can only feel when you are with them. Greg could fall asleep when he hit the chair or bed. Many walk around in a haze, even able to doze while riding the hospital elevator, he said humorously. However, Greg said, he immediately becomes alert when the many serious situations and crucial decisions confront him. I often asked on the phone if he could feel God carrying him along, when he himself was so fatigued. Greg clearly vocalizes his dependence upon God, and could not have gone through those years without our Maker and His everlasting arms holding him up.

And so he continues in his daily life there in Richmond, now as the Chief Neurosurgery Resident completing his sixth and last year when he will be a full-fledged neurosurgeon. Goal: June 1994. He has been offered good positions in several places. Georgia is most promising and a desirable place to live and raise a family. Residency has been a long, and satisfying experience, he says. He loves working with his hands, and using his God-given brain power. During this last editing, he has accepted the position offered by a group of neurosurgeons in Augusta, Georgia.

After three years of residency, one of Greg's statements to us was "I have worked enough hours during my years of medicine to have earned *all* the money I will ever make." That is an astounding, but true statement. He still is earning under $40,000, with many eighteen hour days, and he is 32. (Now, this is 14 years after high school graduation.) He has fewer hours "on call" where he actually stays at the hospital. When on call at Veterans Hospital 24 hours a day for six months, he carried his cellular phone with him, able to keep in touch with the rest of the world. A new freedom was his, but he knew every call was a life or death event to someone who was dependent upon his best and most experienced judgment. The many years of continuous study, research, and experience *do* give a physician and surgeon great confidence. They have a *sense of worth* and *dedication* to their profession of healing, which few people outside the profession understand.

Gregory did not follow in his father's and grandfather's footsteps in becoming a minister. He followed in my footsteps to carry on the tradition in the medical field. I believe those many years observing my experiences as a camp nurse must have impressed him. It seems to me, most young children with the same genetic composition as their parents will model themselves after one of them.

Amy has done a great job of hanging in there, keeping things going, and teaching German on the high school level. Sponsorship of the cheerleaders had been a regular sideline for her for a number of years. She enjoyed the young ladies in her squads, plus the added contact with the mothers. At this writing, she has quit her extra job to return to making crafts and decorating, hobbies she loves and in which she excels, but most of all to tenderly care for their first baby, Reid Walter, born November 28, 1993. Don and I are first time proud grandparents of this long-awaited child of God.

Greg and Amy are now well settled into the Eastern way of life in Virginia. We hear good things about him and his potential for a good future. The long hours of work, and being away from Amy has not been easy for either of them. Hopefully, the financial remuneration will be rewarding in the years to come.

The following year the big event in our lives was Greg's 30th birthday on February 4, 1991. As the day drew near, my thoughts were again directed to his childhood and our life together as a family. I have always felt deeply responsible, as my children's only parent, to document their past for them. What if I died, I thought. It would be lost forever.

How true are the words: "pictures are worth a thousand words!" They could tell me a lot. Those 500 slides I viewed of our past in preparation for his birthday would remind Gregory, not only of the *events*, but possibly the *feelings* of that day. Look in the eyes of our past ... Why not make a home movie of his childhood? It could be viewed in 30 minutes, and would have appropriate music for special events. So that is what I did. It was not a professional job, yet it reminded Greg of how much I really cared about him. I also had a dozen 11 x 17 prints made of his childhood pictures, most of which he did not remember seeing. How much we had forgotten! The memory had too much to hold.

Amy had planned and prepared a fantastic variety of the best foods with the help of their good friend Annette McGhee, who hosted this fine affair in her home. Many friends were invited for this big birthday. What a grand party, even more exciting because it was a *total surprise* for him! We still cannot believe we pulled it off! He did not even find out that Don and I and his Godfather Bob and Lori Duesenberg flew in for this big event. I believe we gave Greg the shock of his life when he opened the door to us! Well, I need not say how much laughter and tears we had that evening. I had viewed the movie of his life so often, I fortunately was all cried out. After all, I said to myself, if I start crying who will narrate? And so after studying every picture hanging on the walls, Greg settled into enjoying family, colleagues and friends that evening. Amy is so talented in cooking and decorating. It was a perfect evening, one that I have thought of frequently in the lonely days that followed.

Life for me has been anticlimactic since Greg's graduation and marriage. Searching for a long-range goal for myself has been most difficult. All my life since having children, has been pretty much directed toward *their* goals. I took my responsibility as a parent *very* seriously. What my sons wanted for themselves I also took on, making sure I was available to take them places, giving positive input, and affirming what they were doing. The satisfaction I have received as a parent is overwhelming! Now that I am no longer *needed* as a parent, what do I do next?

Several short-range goals had kept me quite busy since 1988. The first thing I did was to complete Greg's photo albums and scrapbooks. It helped ease the pain of no longer being needed by him, besides looking back on the past really motivated me for my first book. Reviewing my children's and my past together inspired me to delve deeper, and to document my own childhood in North Dakota.

After I had met Lynnda Cramer in January 1990, I really became excited about the reality of writing my first book. I had a burning desire to do this for a long time. It has been said that you have not lived until you have put the events of your life between the covers of a book. So that is what I drove myself to do. My life was unusual and worth putting in print, I said to myself. Although it cost me a bundle, I felt I could do it with some help and motivation. I feverishly began writing everything in longhand on legal pads taken from hundreds of notes and memoirs over many years! I did not have a computer because I had purchased only one and that was for Greg. Lynda followed with reorganizing the material into chapters, and putting it on the computer. What a team! I did the planning to get this book published with Hi-Tec Desk Top Publishing. This novice had to learn a lot about how to do this! I had wonderful cooperation from their well-trained young people. They have taught me so much, and we did high quality work together.

How satisfying to see my childhood in print! I actually relived my youth on the prairie that winter of 1990. Without electricity, running water, or money, how could my father, a preacher with his city wife and five children, survive on the prairie during the "Great Depression"? It was the kind of life many people experienced during those rough years. I had this constant nagging thought that those days would be lost forever unless I wrote them down. As I stand before groups reviewing this book, I continue to get a great thrill out of talking about those wintery days of my youth on the plains of North Dakota. It always brings tears to my eyes when I talk about the hard times my parents experienced, yet they brought up five children who are healthy and successful.

I will not go into detail on the ups and downs of writing my first book, but I will say this. You have to have a *burning desire* to do it, or you will never finish! One sure thing I will tell you, dear readers, writing books is not for the faint-hearted. It is strictly for pleasure and not for profit!

And so, My North Dakota Prairie Childhood came off the press in June, 1990, just in time for the Leininger family reunion. My family and relatives received it very well. I was thrilled. My past was their past, they told me. Now *we all* have it in print for our future generations. So many people have written notes - even three page letters telling me how much they appreciated my putting in print their life, because it was so much the same as mine during those rough years during the Great Depression! Most of all, I have heard from two grade school teachers whom I had not seen or heard from in over 50 years! Their maiden names were Ms. Ruth Finstuen and Ms. Dorothy Otto. My schoolmates in North Dakota will remember them, I'm sure. It gives me such joy knowing I have shared my untold story with others.

Libraries in North Dakota and the St. Louis area were eager to buy copies. The Missouri Peddlers Craft Shops had several book signings and carried my book during good buying seasons. The four women owners, including my friend, Dorothy Kaiser, have been wonderful in giving my book exposure. After four printings it is now being distributed by Prairie House, as well as being available in Waldenbooks and B. Dalton Bookstores in some states. Waldenbooks now carries it in St. Louis. Concordia Publishing House and Concordia Seminary Bookstore stock it as well.

The Fargo Forum newspaper reviewed my book on February 7 of 1993 (without my knowledge)! Thanks to Joe Hall, Editor of this state-wide paper. It was a wonderful write-up, but the only bad thing was that I did not have enough books left to fill the orders! I was elated when I received a communication from Carl Wickman, General Manager of

Prairie House distributing company in Fargo, North Dakota, offering a deal to make my book available to bookstores. Prairie House set up book signings for me in some of the eastern cities in North Dakota in June of 1993. It was thrilling to meet so many fellow North Dakotans in a different capacity. Some of the city and small town papers did wonderful publicity for me. Naomi Dunavan, Columnist for the Grand Forks Herald has written some superb articles on my book, and also many experiences of what it was and is like living out on those cold, yet beautiful plains. I hope to meet many of these folks again this June of 1994 for book signings in the rest of the state.

Greg and Amy's engagement

Rejoicing with them

Greg's graduation, 1988

Happy Mothers:
Bobette, Lori and Rose Marie

Gregory in his Doctoral stole

Roommates, Dan and Greg

Oettings-Kellers-Kuhns-Brauers
after graduation at Powell Hall

Happy celebrations with
families and friends

letters of congratulations

pfefferneuse cookies!

Trying on his
white coats from his Mom

My first book completed, June 1990, <u>My North Dakota Prairie Childhood</u>.

Graduation party at home

"Woman's best friend" Coco

Our Greg's graduation from SLU School of Medicine, 1988

Ed and Joanne Lanser

Greg and Dad

Greg and Mom dancing away!

Sis Dorothy and I

Lori and I

Inlaws: Louis & Sharon Oetting

Greg and Amy's wedding
June 11, 1988

The lovely bride, Amy

Many happy times!

Brauer brothers singing

Mom and Dad enjoying a toast

My siblings at Bob and Phyllis' Island
Dorothy-Me-Lois-Estelle-Bob and Don

Many guests around our dining room table

Friends
Bob, Lori and Bobette

Dining around our table
Dad Oetting, Gloria and Ros Jensen
Duesenberg family

Christmas 1990
12 of us
Such gemütlikeit

Easter at Lori and Bob's

The Tietjens, Rosemary and the Fuerbringers

Sisters in 1992
Dorothy, Estelle, Lois and me

Bob and Lori's 25th
and our 20th anniversary

Greg and Amy's 5th anniversary

Greg's 24th birthday surprise

Amy and Greg in their lovely home

Greg's neurosurgery residency
6 years in Richmond, Va.

Their first home

Surprise party for Greg's 30th birthday at the McGhees, hosted by Annette and Amy

Duesenbergs - Oettings - Brauers

What joy and laughter!

CHAPTER TEN

My Father's Death
Mama's Widowhood
Love For The Elderly: A Few Letters

As you are that I once was,
As I am you will one day be.

"And ye now therefore have sorrow:
But I will see you again,
And your heart shall rejoice,
And your joy no man taketh from you."

John 16:22

I had always felt quite close to my father. We seemed to have a relationship of understanding and acceptance of the good and the bad part of our personalities. Maybe we were equally strong-headed when it came to what was family, and what was morally correct by the German standards. That brought us to a respect for one another that all my siblings did not enjoy.

As Dad got older, he seemed to consider what I suggested as good, especially when it came to his health. He knew that I, as a registered nurse, had more health information than he, and therefore he listened to me. I felt Dad admired my knowledge of medicine, in which I took great pride. There were not many subjects that men thought women knew about years ago, so it was a point of satisfaction in my life to have (one might say) succeeded in this area.

Mother and Dad came to live with us for periods of time beginning the fall of 1981. The evening hours of life were becoming too difficult for them to endure alone. Retirement worked fine for a time, but Mother, being a lot younger (nine years) than Dad, felt she needed to have her own apartment. What was she to do with Dad? He was content to live with us here in St. Louis.

Mom decided they should move to Wheaton, Minnesota, near Dad's nephews, Paul and Carl Leininger, who were nearer his age, and who also loved to play pinochle. Paul's wife Emma and Mom were close friends and took pride in beating the men in pinochle, an important point for these women. They received a lot of satisfaction just from this game, and enjoyed each other's company to the fullest. However, the emotional task of taking care of Dad alone in Wheaton became too much for Mom.

Within a year she was pleading with me to come and help pack up, as they wanted to return to St. Louis to live with us once again. I did have second thoughts about all this moving, but what to do as an alternative was a question we could not resolve. So back to our home they came. How I yearned for Mother to be happy!

When Mom got something in her mind you could not change it. She did not really know where to go or what to do, and this made her depressed. She did not know how to care for Dad and that was frustrating for her. But Dad had always been in charge, and made all the decisions before he got too old to make them. Now he depended upon her. She just did not have the confidence in herself that she was making the right decisions even though she wanted to make them! She tried, but then she would vacillate back and forth about where to live and regret every judgment she made. We "kids" living in all parts of the country would go crazy with her phone calls. Each of us would advise, as we saw it, but then she would end up making another decision to move which she was sorry about later.

Mother finally made the good decision to move to one of the cottages at the Lutheran Altenheim here in St. Louis. They were needing more security and stability and Dad was tired of moving around. After all, he was 85! The Lutheran Altenheim on McLaran Avenue was only a ten-minute drive from us, and it offered a variety of services with various levels of care.

At first the folks qualified for a separate little cottage, with a short walk to the main building for meals. There was a nurse available twenty-four hours a day. The security of knowing there was help in an emergency was important, plus they still could live independently. It seemed a good setup. We five "children" approved of their move, and so it became "home" for them.

In 1985, after the New Year, Dad became ill with pneumonia. Mom had to put him in the nursing home section for more care. He did not like that one small bit and refused to eat. We were out of town for a four day holiday "away from it all" when Dad took ill. I was shocked at this sudden downward turn of his health. There was no question in my mind that I should and could take care of Dad if he were brought back to his own little home. That is what the nurses and I agreed upon.

Mother and I had a big job on our hands just caring for Dad. He gradually lost energy, and slowly became bedfast. He had been diabetic (as well as Mom) for over 40 years, but his blood sugar was getting out of control. I was in consultation with the doctor every day. The insulin shots were not working. Dad was confused and semi-comatose when he was taken by ambulance to the hospital. We could not do it alone anymore. As much as I felt it important to keep him away from a busy and confusing hospital setting, I finally had to give in. I felt badly, but Mother and I needed more physical and emotional help in this kind of crisis.

Because of great distances, no family members came until they were convinced that Dad was dying. Mom and I kept the family informed of his condition. After tests, examinations, and x-rays Dr. Liebhaber, our family physician, reported that Dad's condition was critical. We called all the family to let them know Dad might die soon and asked if they would please come if they wanted to see him alive. My three sisters, Dorothy, Lois and Tudy, came en masse to be with us. The doctor called us together for a conference report on Dad. The news was devastating. Our Dad had a "ballooning" of one of the ventricles in his heart, called a ventricular aneurysm. He could not have surgery in his condition. At eighty-seven years of age had he not had a long and productive life?

We five women became a constant support for one another that last difficult week. Jewish Hospital staff gave us wonderful emotional care. Social workers were available at all times and checked on our welfare. We women needed each other and clung together on our journey towards Dad's death. Accepting my father's terminal illness was unreal to me. I don't think one can really grasp the reality of having a father all those years, and then suddenly not having one. That still grabs my heart, and brings tears to my eyes. I knew I would miss him a lot. Who else would appreciate me the way he did, or would know what it was to be a Leininger? I was proud of our closeness. We understood each other.

On January 25, two weeks after he had gone to the hospital, Dr. Liebhaber discharged him. He could do no more. Dad was taken by ambulance to the nursing home division back at the Altenheim. The doctor could not say how long Dad would live, but knew that he needed total care. Now Dad had said for years he *never* wanted to end up in a nursing home, like so many of the thousands of members of his congregations whom he visited over his fifty-eight years in the ministry.

But here our father was in a nursing home! He was aware of his surroundings, even though very ill. He said he did not want to be there, and refused most food. But God was with him and would not let him suffer long.

Suddenly, his heart must have literally burst from the aneurysm. Breathing became shallow and slow. Consciousness left him. He was fading fast... Before his last breath, we five women, Don, and the nurses aides working on that floor stood around his bed. With arms encircled around Dad's bed we held each other and prayed the 23rd Psalm together. That very day, after ten hours in the nursing home, Dad breathed his last breath... Our cries of grief resounded through the room. Time stopped. That was a moment precious to us all; one that will never be forgotten. It is a moment that I cannot retell without many tears. It is a time to be remembered, and a time to be felt by everyone who reads these pages. It was the second time I was present when a dear family member died. That pain is one I cannot forget. You may have a time like this sealed in your memory, waiting for release. These are the cherished moments of life that we must leave for our children, grandchildren and others. Thank God I have this book in which to pass it on.

After notifying the rest of the family, we called Pastor Norman Meyer who lived nearby to come and pray with us. He and his wife Elsie, who are close friends of ours, had visited the folks numerous times over the years. They were aware of the situation, and empathetic to the needs of parents. Elsie's Mom had been in the Altenheim more than 10 years. Her father lived only two months in the same nursing home, if my memory serves me right. Amazing, isn't it? These pastors lived such a short time in what they felt was a dreaded nursing home setting, maybe because they had comforted so many infirmed folks sitting around waiting to die. They did not want that for themselves.

The Lutheran Altenheim had a nice cozy chapel where we had the funeral service for Dad. It is a perfect size for the residents whose bodies are viewed one last time. The residents attend the funerals, so they in turn will have this family of old folks to fill the pews for their funeral: an assured, secure system! Nobody likes to die alone. The residents of the Altenheim line up in honor guard form out of respect to their friend who now is in heaven. Beautiful! So Dad had his turn that sunny day in January.

Dad wanted to be buried near his parents and many Leininger relatives back on the North Dakota prairies. The next morning just three of us women flew with his body on his final journey to that prairie he so dearly loved. Mom, my sister Dorothy, and I traveled across the country to Fargo, North Dakota. God was truly keeping us going giving us the strength as eagles, as it says in Isaiah 40:31.

The hearse journeyed to the little town of Cooperstown where the closest funeral home was located. We were met at the plane by a cousin, Chuck Dehoff, who had a large American car. No heater was adequate for the freezing cold of that night. The chill factor, we heard later, was -60 degrees!

The four of us traveled for three hours, but it seemed like an eternity. The windows of the car were so covered with frozen snow that we could not see out. Only our driver could see into the bitter cold, dark, snowy night. Between swigs of moonshine, he spat his tobacco plugs into a small coffee can (which just fit on the dashboard edge!) One sudden braking and its contents would have landed in Mama's lap! She was tired and unaware of her precarious situation. Dot and I stayed alert watching that coffee can intently, an occasional giggle slipping from our chilled lips, as like two little girls from the deep past. Dorothy and I share this priceless memory as we recount those sad days.

Cousin Hazel and Ken Leininger opened their house to us those sorrowful and awesome days. The plains people were experiencing one of those three-day blizzards for which our beloved North Dakota is well known. The second funeral for Dad was the next day. A few relatives, old time friends and former church members from the town of Kensal, thirty long miles away, weathered the snow to come for the funeral that last day of January 1985. Brother Bob, Phyllis and entire family traveled from St. Paul, Minnesota, in the snow storm to see Dad finally laid to rest. Bob's children and other local cousins were pallbearers.

To this day Dad's burial is an unreal memory filled with awe as we watched from the car. Cousin Bill and Alice Rahlf's sons, who took care of the cemetery, lifted Dad's casket with their snowplow tractor and placed it into the frozen ground. The snow was whirling around this overwhelming scene. Men wrestling with the elements to nestle another person into the peaceful bowels of the earth. There is hardly a day that goes by without this hazy vision slipping in and out of my mind's eye. "The strife is o'er, the battle done," says our well known Lutheran hymn.

God shone on Dad that night. The storm had passed, and the brightest moonlight with streams of the "Northern Lights" streaked across the clear, brilliant sky. Breathtaking! We grabbed our coats and took Mama out to see the illuminated heavens. God's power and might *would* truly give us the strength to get through all difficult days! He is Almighty! He is the *Awesome* one!

Mama and I returned to St. Louis alone several days later. Relatives had met us at the airport in Fargo to wish us well. How kind and loving they are!

Upon her return, Mama stayed in the protective and loving care of the nurses and her friends at the Altenheim for the rest of that winter.

The need to grieve for her losses was great. There were so many who would listen to her story, and she to theirs. She developed some close ties there during the winter. Mama and I spent many hours together talking about the past. She had so many feelings of losses. She had yet to mourn for her two sisters' sudden deaths, as well as her parents. She had been so busy being a pastor's wife and raising five children, keeping food on the table and clothes on our backs, she did not have time for tears. How sad! She was void of expressing these emotions. Now I cry for her.

She and I made a very meaningful trip back to her roots in Indianapolis, Indiana, for the second time. The desire to visit the cemetery (St. John's Lutheran) where her parents and sisters are buried was most important to her emotional health. She had not been there for many years, and it seemed to give her a measure of peace knowing where they were at rest.

We also had wonderful visits with the few family members she has, her only niece Inez, and nephew Norman, along with a step sister-in-law Olive, and a few cousins. Mama enjoyed her hours with a couple old school friends too.

It was important for her to revisit her old home and to retell the story and show me exactly how and where her sister Stella was run over by a bus. (The details were given in my first book.) She seemed at peace knowing that I would write her story down, so it would not be lost forever. I taped our conversations of that all important week for her. Thank God for helping me see the necessity for those days for us both.

Later that summer she said she wanted to travel, to visit, and decide where she wanted to live out the rest of her evening years. After all, she was just seventy-nine, she proclaimed, and not needing the extra care of the nursing home. She was healthy, and with her furniture put in storage, she was now free to visit family and friends. It was difficult to be alone and do everything by herself, she confided. Her sadness was profound, but most of all without Dad, she felt like she was "nobody." How could she adjust to not being the wife of a pastor, "The Frau Pastorin" as she was called up there in Canada many years before? She had been a pastor's wife and helpmeet for nearly 60 years. Poor Mama - it tears my heart out to think she felt she was never her own person. She did not know who *Helen Leininger* was, or how she *should* act, she disclosed to me.

The next couple of years she stayed in Seattle with sister Lois and Bill, and then in the nursing facility where Lois worked. She had plenty of folks to share feelings with as she mourned for Dad. We celebrated her eightieth birthday at Lois's with many of her children and grandchildren present.

Mom finally got her furniture out of storage late in 1987 and really started traveling. First back to Wheaton, Minnesota, for a few months, and then a long move into a new Senior Retirement Center in Yakima, Washington. She would be near her eldest daughter Dorothy and her husband Wallace Misterek, who was a pastor in Yakima. This move was appropriate and comfortable for someone like her, who needed to be close to family and to the life of a preacher.

Arthritis was keeping her closer to home these days, and her diabetes needed to be watched more closely. Dorothy, a real exercise and health person was just the influence Mom needed. I admire Dot for her good eating habits and consciousness about weight and exercise. We are all aware of the strong family history of diabetes, and tend to follow a healthy life style. Dot is a good leader and model. She and Wally lead the kind of life in service to their congregation with which Mom was familiar. Wally is very busy as the Vice President of the Northwest District of the Lutheran Church-Missouri Synod. He also is a strong influence for those around him, just the kind of emotional and spiritual support Mom needed. Mama now could happily look forward to heaven to be with Dad. How well I remember when we were children Mom and Dad could sing out "Jerusalem, Jerusalem" with all of us five kids standing around the piano joining in as best we could. Oh, for those bright days of my childhood on the Dakota prairies...

As a child, I did not have grandparents living close by. My Dad's parents died before I was born, and Mom's parents lived so far away in Indianapolis. They died before I was twelve. We saw them a couple times, but I have few memories of them. Maybe that is why my aunts meant so much to me as a child. They cuddled us into their bosoms loving us with hugs during many a visit. Those times I cherish in my memory.

It is said, to know how to grow old is the master work of wisdom, and one of the most difficult chapters in the great art of living. I truly believe this, and each day gain a deeper respect for the aging. My mother when she visited was my priority. The years had taken their toll on her. The arthritis, diabetes and high blood pressure causing strokes whittled away on her body until she at 86 had difficulty with the most natural of things like walking, keeping her balance, and making it to the bathroom on time. These are direct quotes from her, the feelings she had about her body told to me during one of her last hospitalizations. "I feel like a stranger to myself." "My head doesn't want to tell my feet to move." "I don't know which hand I should use." (She was born left handed, but she used to tell us when she started school her teacher forced her to use the right hand, striking her hands with a ruler if she disobeyed.) The memory was still ridding itself of that unwanted material, the trauma. It is painful for me just to write about the anguish she experienced.

When I heard her emphasize to the nurses that "*My* name is *Helen*" I knew she was at long last becoming *someone*. Her memory for specific events was unscathed by time, but her short-term memory was fading. Daily existence was a perpetual chore, searching for things that remained of life's memories and her few material possessions remaining. My heart bursts with sadness at the losses this dear mother of mine was experiencing.

My husband Don has an Aunt Elsa Saxenmeyer who is also one of God's precious elderly. She is yet of sound mind, free of disabling strokes, born just a couple months before the turn of this century! Her ninety-four years do not interfere with her positive thinking, kindness shown toward all people, and unswerving faith in the Almighty God. That wonderful smile of hers continues, even though the body hurts with arthritis and the hearing is all but gone.

She admitted to "slipping" a bit as Tanta Elsa (as she likes to be called) detailed her funeral plans to us one Sunday afternoon. She does not want to be morbid, and as if to comfort us, she says, "I may not be here tomorrow." How wonderful of her to give us fair warning. She does know how much we care for her, dear precious soul that she is. Our conversations over the years with her have been some of the liveliest and sharpest, always current and precise. What a precious creation she is! She loves life and its people, but she is looking forward to that grand reunion in heaven. Even her old Tanta Hannie Stieghorst, who died in 1992, lived to be 105 years old (born in 1886 - imagine!).

Aunt Elsa loves to sing hymns and prayers in German, the language of her youth. Whenever family is visiting, someone starts up the songs and we go on singing many a verse! The following is one of the many verses that grace the walls of relatives' homes. Her brother, our Reverend Uncle Eric Brauer and his new bride, Maxine, have supplied us with copies of these "old sayings" to pass down to our children. I have framed some of these beautiful mottos for the families, and now are on their walls.

"Sind auch die Tage manchmal grau und Schwer Hoch uber Wolken Strahlt ein Sonnenmeer!"

"When days are dark and ominous, remember high above the clouds is brilliant sunshine."

Just recently (1993) there was a wave of elderly nurses who died, fellow Alumnae at Lutheran Medical Center. These were "institutions," married to the nursing profession, yet maintaining some power and control over themselves to the last breath. I feel it important to mention a little about one of them, because of the esteem I held for her. She was a role model for me for over 40 years. She was Miss Katharine Beckmann. One who greatly influenced the lives of aspiring young women hoping to become nurses. She taught "Nursing Arts" for many years, and was my instructor in that course. She was dedicated to nursing, loyal to the institution, and precise in all that she did. Her expectations of us were unequaled; her aspirations for us the highest. We did want to come up to her goals, no question about it, or we did not last. I was always quite pleased when she told me with raised eyebrows and a twinkle in her eye that she was the only instructor who attended *both* of my weddings. She seemed to take pride in the fact that she knew someone who could snag two men, even though she chose to remain single!

These high standards of performance, begun years ago by women like Miss Beckmann and Miss Kubler (who still is active in the Alumni well into her 80's) have been maintained by Lutheran Medical Center graduates. It has come to my attention as the Representative from the Alumni to the School of Nursing, that to this day our nurses receive positive feedback from patients for their empathetic, caring attitude, and good nursing care. It could well be that the teamwork of folks, like the chaplains and social workers, alongside the faithful doctors and nurses, continues to make the difference.

Since 1984 when Gregory entered Medical School, I have had the distinct privilege of receiving a hands-on education on the dreaded disease of the aging, Alzheimers. My former neighbor across the street, my Helen, as I will call her, began to forget, first of all, where she was going when she got into her car.

One evening Helen drove away in that bright, yellow Pontiac, and did not return. Since I was hired by her son to watch out for her and take medications to her, I felt responsible. Fear gripped my heart. Where would she go? How far back in her memory would she be living at this moment? The police were called, and we desperately searched for Helen. Night came and the darkness seemingly had swallowed her up with her yellow car. Fear that something dreadful had happened to her enveloped us. Hours later the police called and said they had found her. Helen was parked in front of her childhood home in the suburbs of St. Charles. Yes, she had gone back to the days of her youth that day.

Dear Helen would return to those days many times in her own mind. Other days she does not remember who I am, but that never keeps her from cooperating with me. She trusts me, though not knowing who I really am. A conditioning. *That* basic feeling of security has never left Helen. Somewhere in the recesses of her mind sits the memory of being rescued from the floor many times, unable to get up by herself; or the time one of her meals-on-wheels was burned when she left it in the styrofoam to be heated in the oven... God was truly watching over her! My affirmation of her personhood, not reminding her of the wrongs she is doing, but of the right things, the positive and good, has made our relationship work. Many times she looks straight at me and says clearly and with deep meaning "I love you." Whatever it is, is not to be defined, but to be understood and accepted. That is all that is necessary.

I am privileged to have cared for Helen, and am a better person for it. She now resides in one of the best nursing homes around, Delmar Gardens, Chesterfield. Her only child, Philip, is a renowned doctor of Nuclear Medicine at Columbia University in New York City. My son Gregory continues to drive that bright yellow car which I bought from him after Helen went into the nursing home. I had it painted a beautiful bronze and it has been serving Greg for a half dozen years.

My only living aunt of the Leiningers is dear Aunt Irene from St. Paul, Minnesota. She is a perky *ninety-eight-year-old* with an active mind and great sense of humor. "I don't even buy green bananas," she says with a laugh. Aunt Irene lives in her own apartment, but her children and grandchildren are near to care for her needs. She is truly amazing, blessed by God in every way.

I look forward to the letters from several of my other aging friends and relatives who are so special to me. I hold onto their letters of the past for years on end. My dear friend, Elsa Zschoche-Neusiis, who had formerly lived in St. Joseph, Michigan, has been widowed twice in the last twenty-five years. Her Martin had a heart attack while driving his car, dying shortly thereafter. Her Frederick died of a stroke a dozen years later. This was the second time she was left alone in a big, old house. She recently moved to a senior citizen retirement home in Fort Wayne, Indiana. Elsa still writes newsy, interesting details of her daily life, her memories, her feelings, her fears. Though her physical health is poor, her brain is sharp. She considers communication with her friends and family a priority, a must. I feel the same way toward those I love.

A communication from my aging friend of bygone days in Michigan:

Ft. Wayne, Ind.

Christmas 1992

Dear Ones:

Thank you for the lovely greeting for Valentine's Day. It meant a lot to be remembered with so much love as I live this solitary life. It is getting better - there are many in my category and we reach out to one another. One goes through this adjustment with each move. I hurt the most when I lost Martin and moved off into a completely different life. Having children and grandchildren close and all the St. Joe friends helped me through the "valley" there. Like the saying goes - we are not strangers here, only friends we haven't met heretofore. Awakened this morning with another heap of snow to look out upon. Ruth cancelled my medical appointment yesterday but she is willing to try it today - taking for granted that the folks out and around have adjusted to the peril of ice and snow. We wilso grab the necessities for the larder. I invented a new word (will also) along the way. Our temperature is very, very low, so with my fur-topped boots and my quilted coat from Anita a year ago I'll be snug, although they make my walking more difficult. -- Your rose card comes, when greetings with the resurrected Savior will be of prime importance. The Lenten season will definitely cleanse me from the feeling I have been deserted. The pure white of the landscape beyond my third floor windows is already doing its bit.

A phone call from Lois, Ruth Hohenstein's sister in Milwaukee, with plans for our Kuehnert reunion did help to give me happy thoughts and fill me with thoughts of this happy being together--end of July into August. There are still four Kuehnerts living, two in the 90's and two nearing that milestone, and God took my mother so early--one day into her 33rd year with five small children and Papa continuing with Grandfather and Grandmother Kuehnert. I wish I had your ability and desire to write about my life's experiences. Much is already getting away from me. I feel very flattered that Martin and I could be a part of your memories. They were of ours, too, and remain with me. I thank God for our years together in Berrien County. Some days I feel that is where I should be now in order to have more contact with my children--Anita and Elaine making frequent contact with the Weimanns. Jerry's drug company has recently erected a drug store in Berrien with Jerry as manager, saving him those 20 miles each way each day.

May all go well with Gregory and his National Board exams. That is his last hurdle I take it. It will--just think who his parents are. Now for a bite of lunch--soup and an apple.

Remembering you warmly...

and wishing you memories of

a very Merry Christmas!

and God's blessings for the New Year.

My love,

Elsa

My elderly cousins, Hazel and Alice from North Dakota, are the great communicators from the Leininger/Rahlf clan. I look forward to each of their newsy letters telling about their lives and families all still in North Dakota. For me it is comforting to know those relatives are still there. Each time I return to those open spaces and bright starry nights, my heart fills with joy, tears well up into my eyes while once again greeting with hugs and kisses the kin of my youth. Here are portions of a couple recent letters from those cousins:

Binford, N. Dakota

April, 1992

Dear Rose Marie & Don,

What a nice surprise to hear from you again! So soon after Christmas!

Every day I look at the temperatures for certain cities in the U.S. St. Louis is one; so I know what kind of weather you are having.

Seeing we have relatives or friends in Denver, Portland, Seattle & Spokane, I read their temps too.

Thanks so much for sending me that history of the Leininger family. I imagine they came from Alsace, Lorraine as that seems to be where the Leiningers originated. Then I guess the branch we are from came to Pennsylvania and spread out from there. I'm sure if they traced things back far enough, there would be some relationship as Leininger is not a common name. I guess there are more of them than we think!

John's and us were at Kay's in Wahpeton Christmas Day. John's went on the next day to Pine City, Mn. to visit his son & family. We were at Kay's five days. James played in a basketball tournament, so we spent three evenings going there.

We were at Karen's New Year's Eve & Day. We would have stayed longer, but Ken had a two day meeting in Carrington that Thurs & Fri, so we had to come home. I usually go with him and visit my sister, who lives in Carrington, but she wasn't home from California yet where she was spending Christmas with her daughter & family.

We had some fairly nice weather during the holidays. Temps mostly in the 30's but lots of fog. We do have some snow. Tomorrow we plan to go to Mitchell, S.D. where Karen's son goes to college. They are honoring the basketball players. There is a reception & then we will go to the game. It is to be 20° below zero tomorrow A.M. so I kind of dread going.

My nephew thinks I should write the story of my life, so my children will have it. Won't be a book though!

I surely really got old when I reached my 80th birthday. I have slowed up so much and it is hard for me to do certain things, especially climb up and down a ladder when I am washing walls and ceilings. My knees are bad.

It takes me so long to get the Spring house cleaning done in this big house. I have the porch, attic and basement to house clean yet. I kind of hold off cleaning the porch and attic as we usually have blowing dust until the fields come up. It usually blows in badly.

We had a very mild winter and not much snow. So we will have to hope for lots of rain this Spring.

Of course we have been so busy going to our grandchildrens' basketball and volley ball games all winter. Now come the Spring activities - track, music contests and speech meets are in full swing.

Love,

Ken and Hazel

Binford, N. Dakota
Feb. 1992

Dearest Don & Rose Marie & Greg:

Kinda late for a Christmas letter but maybe you have heard from some I have written to, that the 2 weeks I usually spend writing them, I spent in the Hospital in Fargo, getting a new knee. I had my xrays & everything long before & had written the Dr. that I was ready to come in, as he told me to, & don't you suppose he forgot me. I was down & had a chiropractic treatment & told the girl there about it. That was Dec already & she called him, so I got to St. Johns in Fargo on Dec 14 & had my knee put in next day. He promised to have me home by Christmas, so I got home late P.M. of the 24th. The Ramseys were all here having an anniversary party for one of their family so David Ramsey wanted to have a candle light service in our church that night of the 24th. He's a Pastor from Canada (Alma's son). It was sure a lovely service & got to visit with them all. I haven't been out of the house since. Back in 1987 we set a record for the warmest year in history & that sure changed when the New Year came in - we went down below zero by Jan 2 & it was below zero for 2 whole weeks. Then on Jan 11 at dark a storm began & kept on till daylight. It was the worst storm that we've had for at least 3 years!

Sure is crazy how things can change. I'm still on this walker but my knee is slowly losing its big size - sure hope it can get back to normal by next Tuesday. That's when my 6 weeks appointment is supposed to be with the Dr. Just have to go to Valley City. He comes there a couple times a week I guess.

Can you imagine what my life has been like. A busy old lady with 5 males to cook & wash & bake etc. etc. for, & then have to sit around - Lucky I had 24 letters to write since then - This is my 25th letter since I started 2 1/2 weeks ago. Had to take things easy the first week I was home & we also had so much going on then. Christmas Eve - some of our older kids came home then - their married kids go to their inlaws. Had a couple younger married grand kids & 5 of those little great grandsons - so cute and were so bashful, but shook hands with Santa. Alice Marie brought over Christmas dinner & all her family were here. You know they live on the Leininger farm where I was born Dec 28, 1905 - before the house was completely finished. Mine, & the twins birthday are Dec 28th -Then on Jan

2nd Bills. They celebrated hers the nite before & then she came on the 2nd in P.M. -Brought enough food for 2 days. She stayed till the P.M. on the 4th. She works in a cafe in Walum where she lives. Is a widow & has 20 grand children - the oldest two will soon be 14 years. With the big family we have, you know we have a crowd for every event. We have 40 grand kids, 52 or 3 great grand & 3 more on the way. All our own kids are all in No Dak except Marilyn who lives in Montana. She taught school there & met her partner. She has 3 married sons - 3 grand daughters & one grandson. We sure are lucky we have these 4 bachelors here at home. Milking their 50 or so cows, have lots more cattle & calves. Farm a few thousand acres of land and are all mechanics. They help neighbors & David hauls cattle to market for any one. 8 married kids in case you may have forgotten. You sure are a busy bunch - some of our daughters & in-laws are involved in so many things too. That's nice, they aren't all like me or it wouldn't be a very interesting world would it? But I'm sure anxious to be on my feet again & back to earning my keep. Am surely glad your Mom has found a place she enjoys. I'm sure it's very hard to lose your mate. Surely enjoyed your letter. Hope mine isn't too boring.

We love you all -

Bill, Alice & Bachelors 4.

It wasn't until 1993 that our Leininger clan came to know the book <u>I Am Regina</u> by Sally M. Keehn, published by Dell Yearling. This book traced the Leiningers back to 1755 in Selinsgrove, Pennsylvania. It was exciting for us to discover our roots went back that far. The book is fascinating. A must to read!

CHAPTER ELEVEN

"JUSTICE FOR ALL" IN THE 1990'S

"These are the times that try men's souls."

Thomas Paine

"With all lowliness and meekness,
With long suffering,
Forbearing one another in love;
Endeavoring to keep the Unity of the Spirit
in the Bond of Peace."

Ephesians 4:2-3

In the year 1992 (when I began this book), it seemed the "old" went out, and the "new" came in on television in politics, and around the world. When Johnny Carson of the "Tonight" show announced he was retiring (after 40 years!) and Jay Leno would be taking his place, other older shows followed. "Bill Cosby" and "The Golden Girls" were just two of the favorites with older stars finally calling it quits. Some shows have many reruns, so we are not completely without their "older" sense of humor and knowledge of the past. These were favorite stars whom our generation had seen since the very beginning of television. I for one sorely miss them, especially Johnny Carson, Ed McMahon and Doc Severinsen with his great band.

The "new" generation is not bad however. Jay Leno is a funny guy and a no-nonsense person. He did well I'd say in surviving the hippie generation without being "too far out." Jay has a band led by Branford Marsalis, an Afro-American, which shows me he does care about racial mix. Both he and Arsenio Hall take care in bringing people of all cultures and walks of life as guests on their shows for us night hawks.

I rarely watch daytime television, but I have seen and appreciated the likes of "Oprah Winfrey" and "Sally Jesse Raphael" in particular. Their subject matter can be interesting and informative. Evening television can be informative with many programs like 60 minutes, 20/20 Prime Time Live, Dateline, Frontline. One can keep up with many things happening in the world.

Bob Hope brought laughter into our home my entire life. His voice rang over the airwaves first on radio and then television. I will never forget that familiar twang as he told one joke after another making us laugh. When life would get the best of us, all we had to do was turn on the radio or television, and peals of laughter would ring through the air. "Thanks for the Memories," Bob. Other family favorites were George Burns and Gracie Allen, Jackie Gleason and Art Carney in the "Honeymooners" and Lucy and Desi Arnez in "I Love Lucy." These people we don't want to forget as they brought joy into so many of our homes during very hard times.

As I look back on the 40 years I have been watching television, I think a lot about Elvis Presley and the negative impression he initially had left some of us. Recently, I read and heard about the good, yet human, down home, sensitive person he really was. He was a lover with a lot of feelings, expressed in his songs. He sang words that expressed the needs of his audience, a majority being women. The need to love and care for others transcends our prejudices, intertwining us with many who are different. Elvis died a lonely, sad man in August 1977, his death as sudden (of a heart attack) as his popularity surge. Interesting how he is idolized, imitated, and refused death by a particular segment of our society.

The graying of the "Baby Boomers" they say is affecting all areas of society. These are the people born after the Second World War between 1946 and 1964. As they move into middle age, they are making new demands on specific industries and on society. Because of their large numbers, they can get what they want. They are an able-bodied group who *can* make a difference in the issues important for the well-being of our whole society. Their era can no longer afford to *criticize* but need to perform, and are doing just that.

They were the "me" generation who "let it all hang out," dropping out of society and rejecting their parents' values. Many parents who raised this rebellious generation are still shrouded in darkness by the pain of their misplaced guilt. This is my generation. Embarrassment and shame, brought on by these wayward children, stifle their lives.

That generation trying to escape reality through the use of drugs and alcohol, with many dropping out of school makes it very difficult for employers to find reliable people. They are looking for educated and trained workers. To get qualified help, corporations and the government has to set up training programs to make more productive citizens. Quick fixes and short term gratification do not work. These "Yuppies" or "Baby Boomers" are fighting the aging process (or whatever words used for that generation), demanding to have everything made just for their self-satisfying appetites. That is one of the reasons we have a multitude of choices in just about everything we purchase, whether it be clothes, shoes, food, or cars. Each has to be available in all colors, shapes and sizes for the demands of this larger generation of consumers.

This generation who rejected the bra and the girdle in the late 60's and 70's now insist on a variety of the very best quality to fit their needs of increasing size as they mature. Many women are having babies in their thirties and even forties along side an increasing need to care for their aging parents. These times too are busy and very stressful for their generation.

College tuition for their children looms in the minds of many. How will many afford college and yet keep up the lifestyle in which they delight: large homes with everything imaginable for their comfort, and for the achievement of perfection which they savor?

The 50% divorce rate among this group has probably hurt them in the worst way. So many of their children are being raised by single parents, others having step-parents, or a boy friend, leaving children open and vulnerable for abuses of all kinds. These are the families we hear about every day on talk show after talk show, reporting the atrocities and abuses in their lives. I heard on television last week that these children of the baby boomers are called "Baby Busters" - born 1961-81. They are 12-32 years of age; many are poor with few job skills, live with one parent or in prison, and are having babies, many without a father. It is apparent that television is used as an open forum to air all the most intimate problems of their existence. They are truly a hurting generation with trials that only God can relieve.

I recently heard on television a "baby boomer's" words about her generation, quote: "We were well-intentioned in social interaction, but used flamboyant gimmicks." I thought that was a mildly interesting understatement! On this particular program, she was pleading for someone to teach her to pray, and lead her to the peace of God.

I have always been told we can learn from history not to repeat our mistakes, but that may not be true anymore. This fatal disease of AIDS is an example of the result of that generation of "anything goes," free and open sex with anyone your heart desires, gratification to the fullest. "Gather Ye Rosebuds While Ye May" seems to be the slogan for some - no bounds nor limits, no responsibility for one's behavior or care for those who may be infected with the AIDS virus. Old diseases like tuberculosis are again on the rise. What a dangerous way to live! We are approaching 250,000 reported cases of AIDS still living in the United States alone (with that same number reported dead since the Human Immunodeficiency virus was identified in 1985). Worldwide statistics say there are 10-12 million people carrying the HIV, and the forecast is for 30-40 million by the year 2000. Frightening figures for those who continue to indulge in the lifestyle to which they are accustomed. AIDS is the leading cause of death among the 20-40 year olds. These statistics came from January and February 1992 reports in the St. Louis Post-Dispatch. This still holds true in 1994.

As a medical person and a school nurse at Lutheran High School North for eight years (until I retired in 1990), I felt it of utmost importance to teach the students as well as the faculty and staff about this deadly disease. I took measures to prevent potential problems in case of hidden carriers of the virus like using gloves, and keeping a 10% solution of chlorox on hand. St. Louis University medical students came to our school specifically to talk about the disease, to field questions, and to quell fears and misconceptions of how the disease is communicated. This dreaded communicable disease is now an integral part of lectures on health in most schools. The word is getting out, and yet, there are so many teenagers who feel nothing can happen to them. They are invincible.

My biggest fear is that my neurosurgeon son, Gregory, is being exposed every day to potentially infected blood. How frightening! Major precautions are taken with double gowns, gloves, goggles and masks, making them look like astronauts walking into the operating rooms, yet nothing is foolproof, they say.

Desert Storm was the war in the Middle East that brought many of us together on our knees praying for one another separated by war. It took only forty-three days in the early winter of 1991 to overpower Saddam Hussein and his thousand Iraqi troops, and get them out of Kuwait. In a masterful plan, General "Stormin' Norman" Schwartzkopf led international troops, and stopped a vicious determined dictator. I liked his statement made later that the U.S.A. was the thunder and lightning of Desert Storm. We had never heard such a clearly visual plan as was laid out on television by General Schwartzkopf. This was his report to the nation, informing us the war was over, and detailing all the events. It was the first war in which so few of our men and women were killed or maimed. Thank God! On the other hand, the vision of thousands of retreating Iraqis, including women and children being killed seems to me an inhuman treatment of the enemy. The news media did the best they could with managed information.

Desert Storm was one of the most fearful of times in recent years. I watched the reports on television every day, frozen to the set, hoping and praying that American lives would not be lost, as in the Vietnam War. Later, General Schwartzkopf received the kind of reception reserved for presidents, they said. It is noteworthy to mention here that

Bob Hope at the age of 88 entertained the troops! What dedication! "We pray this will be the last war, Bob."

That following summer, the door was closed on the cold war, hopefully forever. Churchill had dropped the Iron Curtain in March 1946 with his famous speech at Westminster College in Fulton, Missouri, and now Gorbachev raised it in November 1989 when he ordered his troops to bring down the Berlin Wall. In May 1992 he came to Fulton over forty-five years later to make it official. How exciting! Pieces of the Wall are still being sold today. A large portion of it stands in Fulton as a symbol of peace, never again to have another wall built to separate free people.

Late in 1991 the Russian coup occurred, followed by the dismantling of the Soviet Communist Party. An Arms Treaty was signed with Boris Yeltsin elected Premier of Soviet States. At this point, we were astonished and elated that many more of the people of this world would attain independence, have potentially an open and free market economy, and freedom to vote. Dictatorships will fall, because it is said, nothing which is morally wrong can ever be politically right.

Thirty years after the death of President Kennedy, we have begun to revert back to the extremism of the 60's and 70's. We feel the fight for justice and equality has produced a lot of changes, and we *appear* to be more tolerant of individual rights and differences. However, hate groups, by whatever name, daily are showing up on television and news media reports. The young do not remember other martyrs like the Medgar Evers and the Emmett Tills of the 60's. We must remind our youth of some good that came from the past generation. Our greatest Olympians who have won the gold, like Jackie Joyner Kersee and Carl Lewis, are Afro-American models for all of us to emulate, as well as many others too numerous to mention.

People are saying they want more freedom. So many are tired of being poor. Justice must be given equally to all. Even to the little boy about eight years of age who came to me one evening crying during one of our Parent-Teacher festivals in the 70's. Gus' hurt was so deep that fear showed in every tear that was rolling down his soft brown cheeks. I was so moved by his desperate call for help and the misery he was expressing that I did not sleep all that night. My need to write a poem about this young lad was only surpassed by my inability as a poet. I've searched for the poem everywhere but am unable to locate it. It began something like this: Little boy with pleading eyes came to me in desperation... How I do remember those eyes. I will never forget. The help I gave him was of ultimate importance to him and to me.

The Los Angeles riots in the summer of 1992 gave us a clear picture of the injustice for some, and justice for others. Rage is seen on the television screen in the desperate lives of many people of all races, using guns and knives to act out their angry feelings of unworthiness and low self-esteem. The most vivid analogy to describe racism and the many differences we have as people for me is this picture: It is a scar on society that has been present like the one on my body after my hysterectomy, over twenty years ago. Scarring, called Keloids, generally develops on blacks and blondes. This scar is very itchy, and has frequent sharp pains coursing through it. Extra tissue builds up until the scar is wide and thick. This is like our differences, building and spreading until finally exploding into a painful fury. This is what happened in many of our big cities 25 years ago after the assassination of Dr. Martin Luther King. This is what happened in Los Angeles while I was writing these final chapters. We have come full circle. This is what is happening on our streets today.

We thought we were bringing people together in the 70's and 80's, but that was only a tiny part of what really needed to be done. Self-esteem seminars, workshops and forums for open communication to express feelings on all sides is mandatory. Before we can feel totally comfortable with each other, we must first feel good about ourselves. I am talking about people of all races and creeds. Otherwise our differences like deadly venom threaten to destroy us all.

Violence is a daily experience for many children who relate so readily to the rapper's speech. Many are too far into drugs, alcohol, and violence to hear about the sit-ins and civil rights demonstrations of their parents two, three, and four decades ago. Transforming anger into peaceful change is not an easy task when drugs and dropping out of school are again a priority for many. We people of all races and religion must *work together* and freely live side by side, as I see it, in dismantling the many facets of racism. We have the challenge before us. It affects everyone, let us not forget! Read more in <u>Dismantling Racism: The Continuing Challenge to White America</u>, by Joseph Barndt. This is his second book and he has written many articles on the subject.

People are longing for change, for strong, open and honest leadership like after the "Great depression" and World War II. Maybe some of

Franklin Delano Roosevelt's programs, like C.C.C. camps to put people back to work, would make a difference. The "American Dream" of going to school for a good education, followed by getting a job, having a home, and raising children is now an idea on the brink of disaster.

Alex Haley, author of Roots and Queen gave both blacks and whites a greater sense of pride in America and its history. He sparked a new interest in genealogy, of which many knew and cared little. In the movie "The Color Purple" Miss Celia said "The more things change the more they stay the same." Does that mean we still continue to take two steps forward and one step back?

When we celebrated our Northwoods 50th anniversary in 1990, under the leadership of our highly qualified, first black Mayor, Charlie Dooley, there was a great feeling of oneness and unity in our community. We found the good news that we *all can* live side by side in our communities the hardest to get into the newspapers and on television. Many of us have been tearing down the walls and building bridges for years, but there are just as many around the country rebuilding those walls! How frustrating!

Many churches are now working to address these issues of justice and equality, appealing to folks in the church as ministers of our Lord. Or did He just designate the ordained to this role of serving our fellowman? Maybe when that issue of *serving* one another is clearer, we will be able to see the light at the end of the tunnel on how to deal with each other. The words of "The Battle Hymn of the Republic," by Julia Ward Howe, run through my mind like yesteryear... "Let us die to make men free, while God is marching on..."

A recent visit to the Jefferson Memorial in Washington D.C. again brought to mind the greatness of our forefathers. Etched in stone around the inside dome of the memorial is the following: "I have sworn upon the altar of God eternal hostility against every form of tyranny over the mind of man." If we tend to *liberty* instead of being slaves to money and material things, we will find the answer and motivation for social responsibility, change and freedom. I am hopeful the answer is not still "blowing in the wind" as written by Bob Dylan in the 60's and just recently sung on television by Peter, Paul, and Mary. In Psalm 23:3 we read, "He leadeth me in the paths of righteousness (justice) for His name's sake."

Housing segregation and resegregation have been a large part of keeping the rift between the races alive. We saw it happen before our eyes 25 years ago. It was very sad as well. My former black neighbor, Mami, and I were raking one lovely fall day when she approached me with tears in her eyes. "Why are all these white neighbors moving? What have we done?" As tears welled up in my eyes, I said "Mami, you have done nothing." We hugged each other and I vowed we would never move from that house until old age set in. But I tell you, this does not have to happen. Our City of Northwoods is a good example of how we have been able to live side by side peacefully. Our neighbors Oliver (Bo) and Marion Leslie with their young daughters Allison and Ashley are perfect examples of what makes good neighbors. We have many neighbors just like them surrounding us, who have a different color skin than we have, but that has not made a difference in the quality of our caring for each other. We care for one another as people, as friends. Bo said something to us the other day, which I have not stopped pondering about. "You are role models," he said. This was the greatest compliment he could give us.

"For freedom Christ has set us free;
Stand fast therefore,
And do not submit again to a yoke of slavery."

Galatians 5:1

I have renewed hope for justice as we celebrate the numerous events of the past. The hardest lessons we have learned most surely came from these past 25-35 years. Here is a simple list of the most memorable events I remember, the acknowledgement of a tumultuous generation:

<u>1992</u>

Remember 25 years ago?

The year 1967:

Elvis Presley died.

Woodstock happened.

The Donahue show began.

The Children's Program "Mr. Rogers' Neighborhood" began.

Remember 30 years ago?

The year 1962:

Johnny Carson began with the "Tonight" Show. (Ended in 1992.)

Astronaut John Glenn became the first man in space.

Remember 20 years ago?

The year 1972:

The Vietnam War ended.

The year 1992:

Superman died in the comic books.

Gorbachev officially raised the "iron curtain" with his speech in Fulton, Missouri, celebrating the end of the Communist party in Russia.

Alex Haley's Roots and Queen - related the history and oppression of black Americans in book and television.

Burns - presented the Civil War Series for television.

Bill Clinton, November 3, was elected President of the United States at age 46, our 42nd President and 52nd Inaugural.

The "Baby Boomer" generation came into power. It was in President Clinton's state, Little Rock, Arkansas in 1957, 36 years ago, that nine brave black students integrated the first high school in the United States. Clinton was born in *Hope*, Arkansas.

My beloved mother passed away October 26 on the folks' 65th wedding anniversary. She was buried in North Dakota on Bill Clinton's election day, November 3.

1993:

Remember 25 years ago?

The year 1968:

Dr. Martin Luther King was assassinated.

Robert Kennedy was shot and killed.

Powell Hall was transformed from a theater into a concert hall.

Chief Justice Thurgood Marshall - First Afro-American Justice of the Supreme Court began in office. (He died in 1993.)

Donald Brauer and Rose Marie Leininger Oetting were married August 31, 1968.

Remember 30 years ago?

The year 1963:

President John F. Kennedy was assassinated.

Remember 35 years ago?

The year 1958:

Shari Lewis and "Lamb Chop" began.

<u>Some Noteworthy Events in 1993:</u>

"Dizzy " Gillespie, King of Bebop died.

Sears Catalogue (which began in 1896) ended.

Don and I celebrated twenty-five years of wedded life. Married August 31, 1968.

Our son Gregory and Amy celebrated five years of marriage.

Gregory and Amy had their first child, Reid Walter Oetting, on November 28, 1:05 a.m. Don and I became grandparents for the first time.

"Peter Rabbit" was 100 years old!

The year the "old" generation with George Bush went out, and the "new" younger generation took control of the United States, under President Clinton, Hillary, and Vice President Al Gore.

The song "Don't Stop Dreaming about Tomorrow" was born.

Our City of St. Louis elected the first Afro-American as Mayor, Freeman Bosley, Jr.

The first Woman was appointed as United States Attorney General, Janet Reno.

The Health Care System is being revamped by Hillary Clinton with a large governmental committee.

There are four *living* former Presidents of the United States and their wives:

Gerald and Betty Ford, Jimmy and Rosalyn Carter, Ronald and Nancy Reagan, George and Barbara Bush, and the widow of a former president, Lady Bird Johnson.

We noted the passing of St. Louis greats as radio Bob Hyland and Bob Hardy of KMOX.

The Brady Gun Control bill passed providing for a five day waiting period for handguns.

"The 1st 90 years of Bob Hope" was celebrated on television. He was honored for giving us 60 years of movies and 40 years of entertaining our troops during wars.

Our Pastor Samuel J. Roth and his wife Mary retire from the parish ministry after faithfully serving the Lord for 38 years.

Coming up in 1994:

My husband Don retires from teaching after 35 years.

My Gregory completes neurosurgery residency, and joins a group of neurosurgeons in the historic eastern United States, Augusta, Georgia.

50th Anniversary of our city of Northwoods
Many were honored

Our Mayor
Charlie Dooley

At the podium again or dancing

1st Ward Civic Ass'n Officers:
Fern-Rose Marie-Jack-Lula-Virginia-
Mayor Jim

With my family: Mom-Lois-Bob-Dorothy

Our neighbors, the Leslies:
Bo, Marion, Allison and Ashley

CHAPTER TWELVE

THE DEATH OF MY LAST PARENT, MOTHER
HOPE FOR THE FUTURE:

Celebration of Life

"My brothers (and my sisters), I do not consider myself to have fully grasped it even now. But I do concentrate on this: I leave the past behind and with hands outstretched to whatever lies ahead I go straight for the goal - my reward the honor of my high calling by God in Christ Jesus."

Philippians 3:13-14

"And now abideth Faith, Hope, Love, these three;
but the greatest of these is Love."

I Corinthians 13:13

It gets clearer, the longer you work at it. Or the more you say about what you think, the clearer you are about what you think and feel.

We have gone full circle since Don's and my wedding day twenty-five years ago. I hope and pray I have made a difference in our little part of this vast world, in my pursuit of justice for myself *and* for the people who live in our neighborhood of Northwoods. Just maybe it has made a tiny dent in "freedom for all." They say one can do anything if one sticks to it long enough. That has been my philosophy in working here in our integrated neighborhood, never giving up in bringing our two races, black and white, to a better understanding of one another.

Don's and my love has been put to the test many times over these 25 years, and shaken to the core. The vows we took at the altar of Bethel Church that August morning in 1968 have stood the greatest tests of our times. As we age, the passion may be less, but the conviction to remain strong and tied together has not wavered. We have only God to praise for this blessing.

Remember how you felt when you reached a "big" or "special" birthday in your life? Well, don't think of it as another birthday, think of it as another year spent mastering the intricacies of a rewarding and demanding life. When I reached the big six-0, I crossed over a major milestone into the era of being "older," and hopefully wiser. My Don gave me the biggest party I ever had in my life. He wanted it to be a surprise for me, but there was no way he could master that with my continual presence in the house. He had to consult with me on details. I thought it a nice idea to have several of our closest friends here for an afternoon and evening of sharing, to reminisce about the past, and have a few toasts to our future together.

The day was December 12, 1991, the sun was shining brightly, and it was my first big birthday party. Mother had come just for this special day. It would be her last visit and the last pictures taken of Mother and me together before she had a stroke. It was a special day indeed, tainted only by the sadness of Gregory and Amy's absence. He could not excuse himself from his duties and obligations at the hospital. The distance and cost for a few hours with his Mom was too great. I understood and accepted that.

Greg and Amy called just before the party to ask if I would open the package from them. I unwrapped a fine silk jersey black dress, slim with long sleeves and decorated on the bodice with large roses, gold and pale pink, with the appearance of being made of black hills gold. Gorgeous. It fit perfectly and Amy was so kind as to tell me Gregory had picked it out. How wonderful! I could no longer be sad, even though their presence would have been preferred. Don had already given me a beautiful birthstone ring, a turquoise with diamonds around it! Whoever wears turquoise, it is said, will be blessed with laughter and gaiety; his perfect gift to me.

It was so interesting to note the diversity of people, young and old that attended the party. They were our best friends in the St. Louis area. It did not matter anymore what church was represented, moderate or conservative, student or professor, black or white, Don brought them together that day. Don and I each had a nephew, Martin Brauer and Jeffrey Leininger from Concordia Seminary present; our friends from LSTC (Lutheran School of Theology) were here; our friends from the ELCA (Evangelical Lutheran Church in America) and the Lutheran Church, Missouri-Synod, were present. How symbolic! Our message of peace and love among all people is heeded by many if they are to be our friends. Thank God for them all. Thank God for open hearts.

We had a time for reminiscing about what was happening *60 years ago*. What was the world like? These are some of the reminders:

The Star Spangled Banner was officially adopted as the National Anthem.
Hundreds of "hunger marchers" descended on Washington D.C. They were seeking employment asking for minimum wage

President Herbert C. Hoover proposed a lending agency to aid banks and railroads.

Winston Churchill arrived in the United States for a lecture tour.

Our U.S. population was 124,149,000.
Our average income $1,436.
A three bedroom home cost $4,350.
Gasoline was $.17 a gallon.
Bread was $.08 a pound loaf.
Milk was $.50 a gallon.
A new Ford car was $490.

The Empire State Building was completed, the tallest with 102 stories.

New things on the market:
Birdseye Frosted Food
Bisquick
Clairol hair dye
Alka-Seltzer

Best movie: "Cimarron"
The best actor was Lionel Barrymore.
Best actress was Marie Dressler.
Kate Smith and Bing Crosby were big on radio.
"Little Orphan Annie" serial made its debut on radio.
"Dick Tracy" comic strip began.

Tunes that were popular:
"I Don't Know Why"
"I Love a Parade"
"Just One More Chance"
"Love Letters in the Sand"
"Mood Indigo"
"Of Thee I Sing"
"Prisoner of Love"
"Sweet and Lovely"
"Dream a Little Dream of Me"
"All of Me"
"Heartaches"
"Come to Me"

Interesting to note all the tunes were about *love*. I am happy to say I can sing a phrase from each one. Now don't you think a little baby lying in his or her bassinet could really get "tuned in" to music when Mama turned on the radio while she was busy cooking, cleaning and tending to the children? They say music does trigger the memory. If you have music you have "Roses in December" in the evening of your life. This I pray I will always have. It had to affect this little child in a positive way, that love of music and that love of love. Just musing... Last year 1993, we had "roses in November" when our first grandchild, a grandson, Reid Walter, was born on November 28. My heart is full of joy and praise to our Heavenly Father for a *healthy* boy, 7 pounds, 9 ounces! The same birth weight as his father 32 years before!

My birthday party started at 2:00 in the afternoon, and ended when the last friends left at 11:00 P.M. It had been a wonderful day, food was catered and champagne and punch imbibed. Don had done well. What a guy! Now all that teasing over the years about my being older than he made little difference to me. At least I made it to 60! What a relief!

As I said, it was most important for me that Mama was there that day. She deserved my special thanks for bringing me into the world and for being the supportive person she was. She was so proud that I publicly gave her the credit she so deserved. It will be a birthday party forever etched into my mind as it was the last time my precious mother, Helen, would visit us.

Mother had been falling quite frequently, but fortunately all the calcium with vitamin D over the years kept her from breaking any bones. Silently there were clots forming in the brain causing blockage in the back of the neck and head (center of balance). As these falling episodes became more frequent, she eventually required frequent hospitalization.

It was the end of March when I flew across the continent to be with Mother. During the three weeks with her at sister Dorothy and Wally Misterek's home in Yakima, Washington, I supervised Mother's care twenty-four hours a day, even having a few laughs with her at the frustrations and challenges of her learning to walk with the assistance of a walker. Just once, Mama fell backwards with the walker on top of her when I was alone with her. How inadequate I felt in helping my own Mother. I could not lift her (with my own bad back) off that floor. We must have struggled for a half an hour before we both mustered up the strength to get her onto a nearby chair. We were both in tears by then. I lived her illness with her, truly appreciating the knowledge of the body's failure to improve. It had worked well for eighty-five years, but now it was worn out.

The doctor had said she needed a supervised atmosphere, but we were reluctant to take her out of her own home at the Suntower Senior Citizen Apartments. After days of consultation with family and many prayers, it was decided that Mother would be best cared for in the beautiful assisted living facility in Vancouver, Washington, where my sister Lois was employed. It was a big change for Mother with a difficult adjustment. Having to make new friends was a difficult task for her.

After Mother was hospitalized several times again with increasing disabilities, she required nursing home care. It was a pleasant home just a few blocks from Lois and Bill's home in nearby Camas, Washington, Suburb of Portland.

I flew to Portland in July spending many hours of quality time just being with her - reading and praying; nothing more was needed. She was in God's hands. In the last days of her life, she was no longer worried about the past or the future. She was content, said very little, and smiled frequently though unable to walk. God was truly carrying her all the way. We looked forward together to her ultimate peace in heaven, joining Dad, and the saints who were awaiting her homecoming. She was able to talk about it at long last.

On October 26, 1992 she was reunited with Dad in heaven on time to celebrate their 65th wedding anniversary together. How can we be sad at such a reunion!

The feeling of loss is poignant yet today...

Over the year it became a sharp reality how much Mother meant to me. It was an overwhelming feeling, a void that cannot be filled. She was at eighty-six, the last of six parents.

My heart actually began fluttering and feeling like it was continuously turning over in my chest the day we were notified of her death. It was a scary feeling, but so real. What else would your heart do at such another loss? It seemed quite appropriate actually, but then it continued day after day. Why could it not just quit grieving for a moment, as I was getting very tired and anxious? My grief seemed locked within the walls of the arteries, pushing and pressing to burst forth. Finally reality hit me. I took out my sphygonomanometer and stethoscope to check my blood pressure. Well, I need not tell you it was up to 175/102, then down to 160/100. I hurried off to my friend, Dr. Liebhaber. I felt I might die. This went on for days as I took increasing doses of blood pressure medication ordered by the doctor. He then referred me to my former cardiologist who ordered the gamut of heart tests.

Well, the bitter pill is accepting high blood pressure, extra beats, and a mitral valve prolapse which does not get better. Heredity or predisposition to the problems of previous generations has just been passed down to me. I was not only feeling the loss of my mother, but also the loss of perfect health. A sister and brother have recently acquired diabetes, but I have thus far escaped that malady. The pain in my neck and back has nothing to do with heredity, but an unnecessary risk I took over 15 years ago. Have you ever laid on an innertube pulled by a speedboat? Well, do not. I did, and I have had frequent bouts of sudden pain anywhere down the spine any time. With great care and little medication, I still thank God for each day I feel good.

Mom was laid to rest in North Dakota beside Dad. It was November 3 (and election day for Bill Clinton). Nearly seven years ago we had made that unforgettable flight to the great plains to bury Dad during a blizzard - the cold and winds of 60° below; now mocked by another snowstorm, the first of the season. Unbelievable, but true.

Again, only the close relatives and friends risked the cold and winds of those prairies to celebrate mother's heavenly entrance. My three sisters, brother and his wife, and two grandchildren came from all parts of the country. Our dear 98-year-old Aunt Irene Leininger and cousins Warren and Lenore from St. Paul picked me up at the airport in Fargo. I had flown those miles in a twelve-passenger plane which I felt sure might not get me to my destination! Hazel (at 81) and Ken (Leininger) with food donations from others, fed fourteen weary people at their table that night, and weathered it all with nary a complaint.

The next day it was still snowing, but Mother was buried anyway. The service was beautiful out there in that little church in the country of Zion, Binford. We four sisters, Dorothy, Lois, Estelle, and I along with my brother Bob and family, Phyllis, Anna and Jim, followed Mother's casket, carried by the older generation of cousins proud to do their final deed of love, out to the cemetery behind the church. The cold winds and snow so familiar to all swirled around us. We stayed to see her casket finally lowered into the ground. It was so frozen, the opening for the casket had shrunk making it difficult to fit the vault into the opening. I recall thinking how strange... It took numerous attempts, after removing dirt, before it finally fit into the ground. Then... out of the recesses of my hazy mind came an earthly groan - like a moaning deep from the soul. I heard it that day as we watched in frozen silence... I lowered the spray of flowers gently on top of the casket, hesitating for a time... Reluctantly, we walked silently away. Mother was now at peace.

My cousin with multiple sclerosis died and was buried in that same cemetery two days later. It was still snowing, but we went to see him at rest. Praise God for the many relatives who have great endurance, and no fear of the weather. They lend a special emotional and physical support. The snow had stopped, but the big plows had not come through those small country roads. Several cars got stuck upon returning home. It wasn't until our return trip from my cousin's funeral that we got hung up in the deep snow, the first time this winter, Hazel added.

The large plows will come through to be sure, I was told, because deer hunting season begins the next day! Sure enough, that is a *major happening* on those prairies. The roads were cleared of snow; the hunters, some twenty or so spread out in a straight line across the fields, no way for the hunters' feet to miss the crouching deer in the prairie grass covered with snow. Young and old participate in this sport assuring many families of venison for the cold winter months ahead.

I returned alone to St. Louis a week later. Hazel and Ken took on a parenting role for me. Mom and Dad were both safe in the haven of the prairie earth. I left in peace with God's help. Recalling many times my favorite passage from Isaiah 40:31, "They that wait upon the Lord shall renew their strength. They shall mount up with wings like eagles; They shall run and not be weary; They shall walk and not faint." When I look back on those six days (November 2-7), I feel the warmth and love of our many cousins that kept me going. Only God gives those special qualities of expression to those we love so dearly.

Don and I celebrated our 25th wedding anniversary in July of 1993 (actual date August 31) just so some of our family could be together. It was such a special day full of love and peace. We began the day in church, followed by cake and coffee served by Don and me to our church community who are dear to us. Later in the afternoon, our friends Bob and Lori Duesenberg opened their lovely home for a first-class party given by our Greg and Amy in our honor. About 65 people came on this warm, sunny day to wish us many more happy years together. What a joy it all was.

The decorations were breathtaking, with lovely large bouquets of fresh flowers carefully placed around the house - all planned and completed by Amy. A large variety of gourmet dishes were made for the most part also by this talented woman whom our son married.

My dear Don surprised me with the song "Rose Marie," accompanied by our friend and faithful pianist, Ronald Krausch.

The past was not talked about that day. Don and I wanted only to look toward the future, hopefully with many years of pleasure together.

After the party was over, our Gregory supervised the massive job of cleaning up with the help of Amy's parents and our dear friends. With joy in our hearts, we thanked God for loving and talented family and friends.

Recently, I went to the funeral of Dr. Fred Mortensen, my late husband's doctor. I felt it was important to say my final goodbyes to a person who had changed the course of my life immeasurably. I needed his family to know that I did not hold bad feelings toward their husband and father. And so my faithful friend Lori and I went to the service.

It was a day not unlike the day of Walt's burial, thirty years ago. The family was so kind and gracious. We went to the same cemetery, Our Redeemer, to see him buried just up the hill from Walt. Lingering at the grave was his wife, Diana, and son, Eric. Again, I joined them, feeling compelled to comment on the irony of the closeness of our loved ones' graves. I added that I had forgiven all, if there was anything to be forgiven. Their father had "pulled the plug" so my husband could die. Eric put his arms around me as he lifted two red roses off his father's casket. We walked arm in arm down the hill, and placed the two roses on Walt's grave. It was a final gesture of love and forgiveness, symbolic of the meaning of life...

Mama had a successful life. When it comes to counting descendants, God had richly blessed her with five children, eighteen grandchildren, and nine great-grandchildren. When these children and grandchildren read these pages, I want them foremost to know about the past and some of the experiences of the generations before them. I want them to know how generously love was given, and for them to pass it on.

As we stand on the edge of the 21st century, I have hope and optimism that this generation will look back at the appalling injustice and inequities that existed in my time, and will also work for the same principles of justice for all. Foremost, I wish for a renewal of peace and responsibility among all people. Their continued dependence upon our Lord who always gives them the strength and courage for each day. He will help you be a blessing to others as you attend church. Therein is love. I will continue doing the things I do best, with people, staying involved. My interests have been the same for me these many years; as a Ward Coordinator in my neighborhood, as an Elder, Reader, and Server in my church, as an Alumnae Representative from the School of Nursing; playing bridge with friends, golfing at Holiday Island, in

Arkansas with Greg and Amy, and spending a lot of time loving my new grandson; many family reunions.

I look forward to the ordination of the 4th generation of preachers in my life time. Numerous weddings of 41 nieces and nephews in the Leininger, Oetting and Brauer families are evolving into a generation of grand nieces and nephews. The unending cycle of life...

Through this book I have learned to know myself better and have shed many tears. I have seen where I have been, and the way I will go in the future. To know myself is to understand others. Remember me when you hear these words:

Love, hope, optimism, endurance, peacemaking, justice, affection, music, strong faith, dependence upon God...

A German saying written by Goethe hangs on our wall:

"Each day one ought to hear at least one little song,

read one good poem

behold one outstanding piece of art,

and if at all possible, speak at least a few sensible words."

This I will try to do.

When you have a spare moment, do read Revelations Chapters 21 and 22. It describes so beautifully what heaven will be like - what a day we can look forward to with ecstasy and great anticipation!

As I close this final chapter, the birds are chirping, many flowers are blooming, and the grass is turning green. Summer is not far away; but now it is spring with all its beauty. The trees look especially green this year, even the flowers are so beautiful and intricately made, when I look closely into their little faces. God's creation is so wonderful. Each of us is here to enjoy the gifts he has given... I search for the beauty in these things more intently these days. One can find loveliness in the faces of those lives touched by our care - just *look* for it. Life will not be easier these next twenty or so years that God will have me live on this earth, but just maybe with renewed wholeness I will be freer within myself to laugh, to love, and to accept love. I pray that God will grant this to me. There were times last winter with Mother's deteriorating health, that I feared I surely would clear all these notes away and never return to them again. The gift of enduring these pages also was given to me.

Just putting the past on paper has been a healing experience; I have learned so much from reliving these times. Many of you who have read this book will identify with many things. These events in life will ring a familiar bell and you will have found a release of the forgotten past. You may say, "Ah Yes, this is the way it was for me, too."

Duesenbergs at home before
Kirsten and Bill's wedding

Don doing what he likes best:
at the organ playing for nieces and nephews
weddings accompanied by brothers
Paul and Fritz

Music, Music, Music
Around our piano
singing and playing

On the beach

At our old organ

Good friends:
Miriam-Me-Shirley-Rhea-Sandy-Donita

Habitat for Humanity-Blitz Build
Volunteer nurses, July 1994

Friends at the Lansers
Thelda-Me-Marie-Joanne

Zion in the country near
Binford, North Dakota
Mom and Dad buried here

Don and my 25th Wedding
Anniversary, 1993

Brauers in Monango, North Dakota, 1994
Don-Me-Roland-Pinky-Paul-Lois-
Fritz-Ann-Hank-Carrie

Many games of "Oh Heck!"

Mama's big birthday!

Birthday celebration with
family and friends

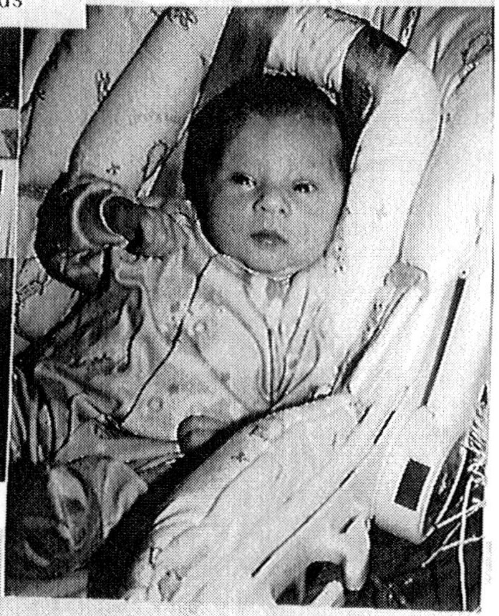

Our precious only grandchild,
Reid Walter Oetting, born Nov. 28, 1993

Mama and I
on my big birthday

Reid wearing his Daddy's
clothes 33 years later!

Greg and Amy's 5th
Don and my 25th

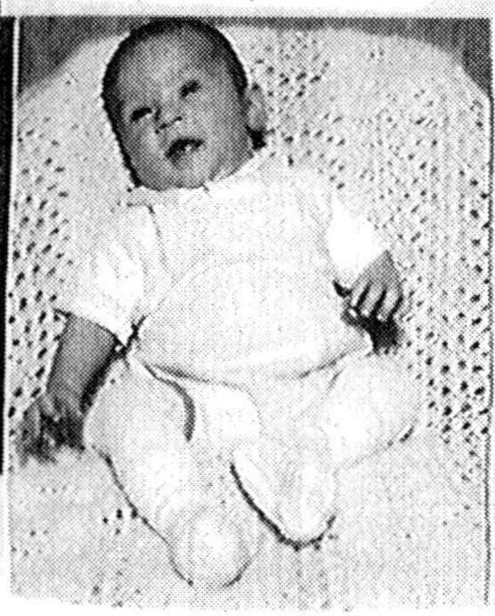

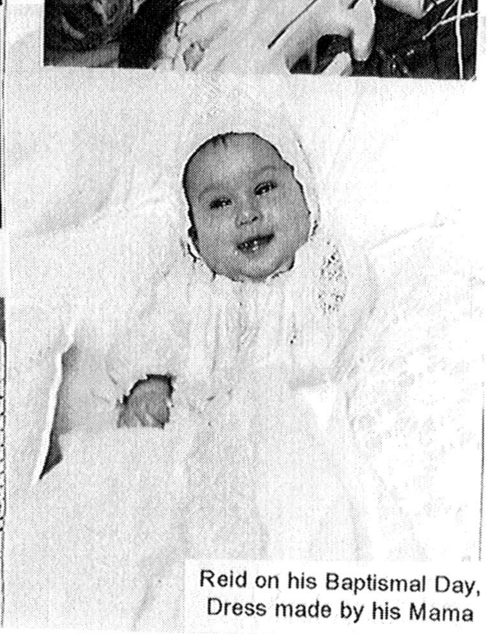

Reid on his Baptismal Day,
Dress made by his Mama

Places we frequent

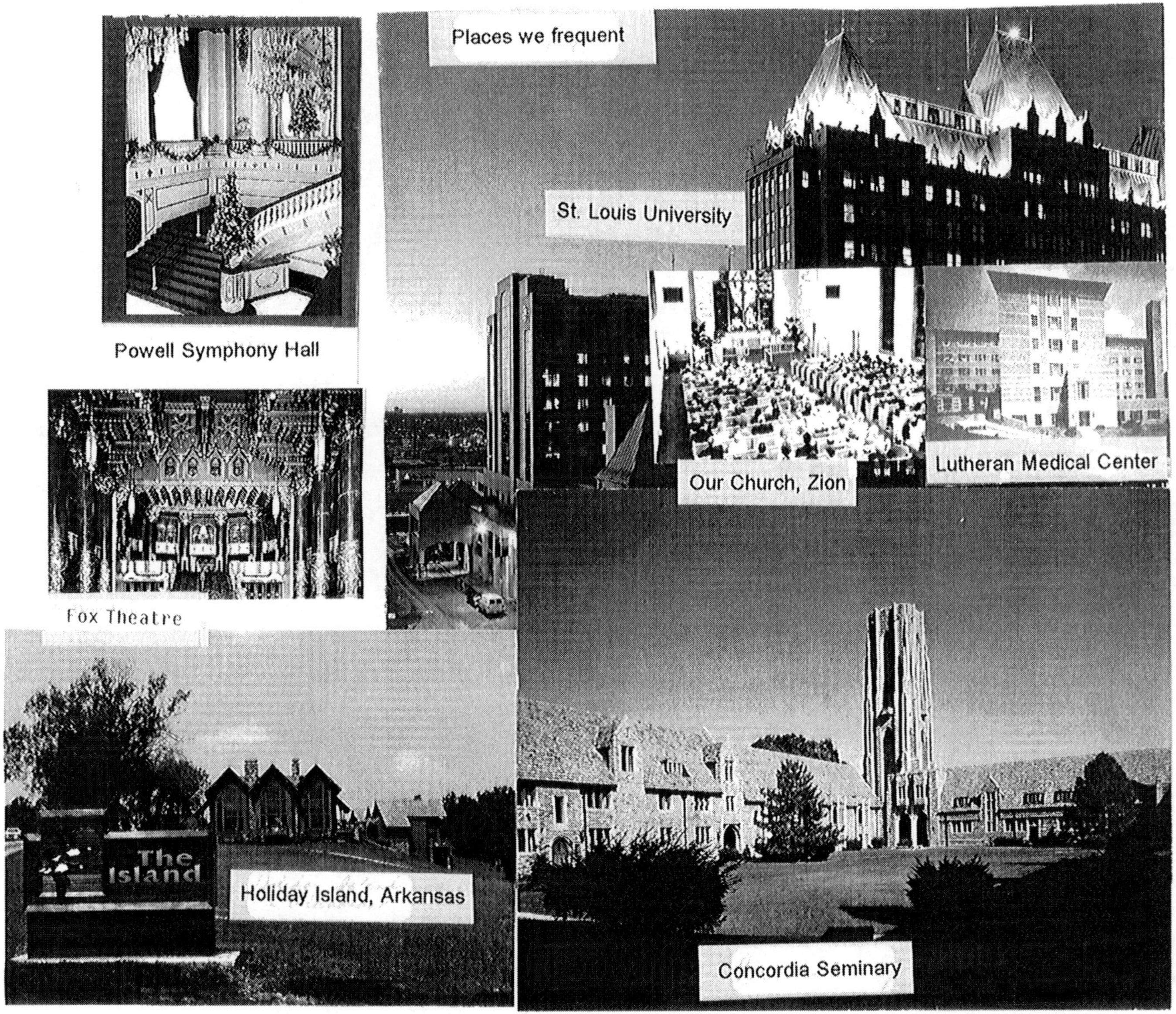

Powell Symphony Hall

St. Louis University

Our Church, Zion

Lutheran Medical Center

Fox Theatre

Holiday Island, Arkansas

Concordia Seminary

MELLOWNESS

"I like spring, but it is too young.
I like summer, but it is too proud.
So I like best of all autumn;
because its leaves are a little
yellow,
its tone mellower,
its colors richer.
And it is tinged a little with
sorrow.
Its golden richness speaks
not of the innocence of spring,
nor of the power of summer,
but of the mellowness and kindly
wisdom of approaching age.
It knows the limitations of life
and is content.

Lin Yutang

EPILOGUE

It is my great desire, my desideratum, for all of us to live together in peace and tranquility, knowing that there is a God, powerful, yet always loving who is beside us. The God who never leaves us when the hours are trying and the darkest nights of sorrow seem to swallow us. He is there BONDED with us FOREVER. The 'Desert Peace Rose' is the eternal symbol of that true love to which we aspire; the love of our Heavenly Father mirrored by us, and expressed in our daily living: our love toward one another.

So let the passion of that rose burn within, bringing peace and justice to every person not only in May, but in the Decembers of our lives.

Soli Deo Gloria